1

To

Sharon, my wife

Thank you for your love and encouragement

INTRODUCTION

By

Kathy L. Murphy- The Pulpwood Queen

As the founder of The Pulpwood Queens and Timber Guys Reading Nation, there are some people you meet that are of great importance in our world of reading. There are people you are destined to meet, because they too understand the power of the written word. Kacey Kowars is one of those people. I met him during the early days of running my book club. He was interviewing and documenting author's words for online viewing. I was trying to connect readers and authors together with my "meeting and discussing" book clubs (that now numbers over 750 chapters, both here and abroad.) Kacey was connecting us by sharing the author's words from their very own lips through The Kacey Kowars Show and his books.

Why is this so important? I have always felt that bringing an author into the picture of reading a book was to bring that picture into full focus. To read a book is like snapping a photo, you have brought in your own life's experiences and education into the read and "photo" for you to see. To bring that read to a book club discussion, you shared that photograph, and now have various people from all walks of life bringing in their story and understanding into the discussion. But to have an author speak to your book club, or be interviewed by a seasoned book reader, educator, and professional is to truly experience that book. Your photograph has come into full focus, clarity, and understanding.

Kacey Kowars has become our nation's "Keeper of the Words." No one can tell your story better than you and no one can share that author's story better through his interviews than Kacey Kowars. Because Kacey has gone to such incredible lengths to interview our country's finest writers we now have a treasure trove of American letters at our fingertips that give us the entire story. We now know the process that writers like Jeannette Walls, Michael Connelly, James Lee Burke, and (yes) Horton Foote, use to create their literary "photos." Kacey has chronicled the stories of over 100 important writers. This book is just the tip of the iceberg.

Over the years I have often been astounded by the questions that get asked at our book club discussions. The reader often misunderstands the intent of a particular passage of a book- not because they are not great readers- it is just unfamiliar terrain for them. To have the writer explain the book to them in their own voice is truly enlightening. Again, no one can tell your own story better than you can.

The importance of documenting these interviews is extremely important in our worldview of literature. I know there are many people and organizations that interview authors. Some go on to create videos and shows for online viewing, television, or cable. To put the actual words down on paper requires tremendous effort and tenacity. Kacey

Kowars goes beyond the "call of duty"; he has created his own genre of literary criticism. That is why Kacey is the KING of what I call "Keeper of the Words."

Many, many years have passed since Kacey and I met, but it was inevitable that we would meet and become friends, because we share the same desire to get our authors words into the hands of readers everywhere. What Kacey has done is a blessing for us all and is of particular importance to those people who study an author's work.

I give the highest praise by being The Pulpwood Queen to bestowing the "Five Diamonds in the Pulpwood Queens Tiara" to Kacey Kowars. Our motto is "where TIARAS are mandatory and reading our good books is the ONLY rule!" I am thankful for Kacey

Kowars and his lifetime commitment to promoting authors, books, literacy, and reading.

Now it is time to read the words of those that enrich our lives with such great wisdom. I present to you "Another Celebration of Words." I have always said, as The Pulpwood Queen, "Don't we all deserve to wear the CROWN!" and nobody is more deserving than Kacey Kowars. He is at the top of my list.

Kathy L. Murphy, artist/author of "The Pulpwood Queens' Tiara Wearing, Book Sharing Guide to Life" and Founder of The Pulpwood Queens and Timber Guys Book Club Reading Nation

Part One

THE GLASS CASTLE

Jeannette Walls

I met Jeannette Walls in January 2006. Her memoir, *The Glass Castle,* had been published in March of the previous year. The book was already a bestseller when I met her, well on its way to becoming a publishing phenomenon. The memoir stayed at, or near the top, of the New York Times Best Seller List for 251 weeks. Oprah Winfrey named it one of the Top 25 most addictive books she has ever read.

I was invited to attend The Pulpwood Queen's Girlfriend Weekend in Jefferson, Texas in the fall of 2005 by Kathy Murphy, the founder and head of The Pulpwood Queens, the world's largest book club. I had become good friends with Kathy after I started my website, The Kacey Kowars Show, in June 2004. I interviewed Horton Foote, the man who wrote the screenplay of the Academy Award winning adaptation of *To Kill A Mockingbird* in the fall of 2004. The interview was aired in December 2004. Kathy loves *To Kill A Mockingbird* (who doesn't?), and she loved my discussion with Mr. Foote. We talked on the phone for an hour and became instant friends.

Kathy and I have the same goal, to promote authors we admire and to help them sell books and expand their market base. I have met only a handful of people that are as passionate about books as I am, and Kathy is one of them. I clearly remember Kathy calling me and inviting me to the Girlfriend's Weekend, her annual celebration of books, that is now well into its second decade. She was aware that I was a male and I asked her how many men would be attending. She told me there would be less than 10 men out of the 500-700 attendees. My interest was piqued.

   She went on to tell me that Jeannette Walls was one of the featured speakers at the conference, and that she would love for me to interview her. I had not read *The Glass Castle*; my specialty is the American mystery and crime novel. One of my goals with the website is to interview a cross-section of writers- I had already interviewed poets, playwrights, and screenwriters- so interviewing the writer of a memoir made sense to me. Oprah Winfrey had selected James Frey's *A Million Little Pieces* in September 2005. Shortly thereafter, Frey was uncovered as a fraud, leading to one of the most swift and interesting literary downfalls in publishing history.

The memoir was quickly becoming a popular literary genre. Readers have always loved biographies and autobiographies. The year 2005 was an important year in the history of the memoir genre. The memoir was exploding; readers were drawn to the darker side of people's lives. Perhaps it was an after-effect of 9/11; people wanted stories that were over-the-top, different than the lives they led.

Augusten Burroughs wrote several memoirs that reached the top of the bestseller list. His most famous book, *Running With Scissors*, was published in 2002, and was adapted into a movie of the same name in 2006. Burroughs' memoir was also fraught with controversy. He was involved in a court case filed by a family claiming he used their story in his memoir, and that he greatly exaggerated the details of their lives. The case was settled and *Running With Scissors* would be continue to be categorized as a memoir, but the acknowledgement page was changed to reflect the Turcotte family (the litigants) and the fact that that some details were exaggerated. Burroughs felt vindicated by the settlement, and his books continue to sell well today. The challenge of what constitutes 'memoir' and what constitutes 'fiction' has always proved challenging to publishers (and readers).

I drove to my local Barnes and Noble store and bought a copy of *The Glass Castle* (it was still in hardcover). I started reading it and I could not put it down. I read it in two or three sittings. I was mesmerized by Jeannette Walls' story. Our lives had many parallel lines, but there were many differences as well. We were close to the same age, had alcoholic fathers, and kept our personal lives private, fearing rejection should our friends know the truth about the true origins of our family history. Walls is an extraordinary storyteller. She combines pathos with humor, giving readers an honest look at her family. Her use of humor (which gives the memoir its optimistic perspective) is critical to the understanding of the story. Had she told the story from a more serious, blaming tone, many of the passages would have been too painful to read.

I called Kathy after I read the book and told her that I wanted to meet Jeannette and have dinner with her; that I definitely wanted to interview her for my show. Kathy told me should could arrange that, and she did. I did not take my recording equipment with me (it

16

was not a digital world in 2005, I recorded my interviews on a dual-cassette recorder with two microphones and a mixer). The equipment was heavy and cost over $250 a week to rent.

I flew to Shreveport, Louisiana in January 2006, rented a car, and drove to Jefferson, Texas. What a weekend! The town was filled with enthusiastic readers and writers. It was like heaven. Kathy Murphy knows how to throw a party, and this was the first time I had ever been to a weekend book party. The emphasis was on the books, not the partying. Everywhere I went I ran into book lovers. At times it felt like an episode from "The Twilight Zone". It would not have surprised me at all to see Rod Serling step on stage during Saturday night's "Big Hair Ball" and deliver one of his brilliant soliloquies about the importance of celebrating books (and the eccentricities of the readers who were obsessed with authors).

I met Kathy and got settled into my hotel. I had dinner with Jeannette Walls and several other Pulpwood Queen members the first night. Ms. Walls was gracious and charming, very humble. She was genuinely interested in hearing everyone's story at the dinner table. She was not yet a superstar, though looking back today (eleven years later) I was confident that success would not change the person she was. She had overcome too much adversity to fall into the 'success trap'.

She talked about writing the "Gossip Column" for MSNBC, and how she was likely going to give that up now that there were more demands on her time. In January 2006 she had no idea of what was to come. No one did. Few books ever stay at the top of the bestseller list for five years, but that was what was happening to her. By the time I interviewed her in March of that same year she was well on her way to becoming a celebrity herself.

I saw Jeannette the next day and told her about my show (Kathy had told her about it). She was genuinely interested and had looked at the list of authors on my website. We exchanged phone numbers and email addresses. She gave me the name of her publicist at Simon & Shuster. I called the publicist and arranged for an interview after I returned home to Columbus, Ohio. I left Jefferson, Texas feeling energized. I felt, once again, that the path I was following with my website was leading somewhere. I was not sure where, but I was enjoying the ride.

I was transitioning from being a stockbroker for 25 years into working as a fundraising consultant for a major health care company in Columbus, Ohio. Being a consultant allowed me free time to develop my website. I was very lucky; the timing was perfect. Bookstores were beginning to struggle, helping my interviews reach a wider audience. Authors were looking for ways to promote their books that went beyond the traditional book tour. Book tours are expensive, and the major chains were cutting back on the number of signings they allowed each month. I created a 'virtual book tour' that cost the authors nothing; offering them a product they could use on their websites. I caught the 'perfect storm' of technology and content.

The interview I did with Jeannette Walls lasted just over 30 minutes. It received a great deal of attention. Today, in 2018, the interview is featured on a website for teachers, teachingbooks.net, and is used by high school and college students all over the country as a primary source for term and research papers. I have received letters from all areas of the world asking me questions about the interview and asking for my permission to use it as part of a research project. The answer is always yes. It has been listened to tens of thousands of times since 2006. I had no idea in March 2006 that within the next eighteen months I would become a high school English teacher, and that I would be one of the first English teachers in the country to teach *The Glass Castle* as a part of my curriculum. Serendipity.

I am lucky to teach at a school that allows me great latitude in choosing the reading lists I use in my classroom each year.

The first book I added was *The Glass Castle.* My administrators trusted that I knew what I was doing. I learned quickly that 16 and 17-year-old students love this book, they can relate to the craziness of the Walls family.

Over the past 12 years *The Glass Castle* has joined the short- list of the most popular books taught in AP classes in high school and in creative nonfiction classes in college. In 2015 The American Library Association choose the three most widely used creative nonfiction books for educators: they are *Unbroken* by Laura Hillenbrand, *Angela's Ashes* by Frank McCourt, and *The Glass Castle* by Jeannette Walls.

I began teaching the memoir during my first year in the classroom. The book was still on the bestseller list. One way English teachers can create excitement in the classroom is to put great books in the hands of their students. I teach juniors in high school. Most of the books they have read are part of a classic list of novels (as it should be). But I looked at the reading list the teacher before me had used and I pruned it. I covered the same topics; I just updated the book list. I trusted my experience as a reader and a book critic to make the books more interesting to read.

I added Tim O'Brien's brilliant book about Vietnam, *The Things They Carried,* and deleted Joseph Conrad's *The Heart of Darkness.* I had my students read *A Lesson Before Dying* by Ernest Gaines, using this 'modern classic' published in 1993 to replace *Uncle Tom's Cabin.* I had studied with both Mr. O'Brien and Mr. Gaines at The Sewanee Writer's Conference, so I knew their work intimately. I quickly learned that if I was not passionate about a book I could not expect my students to love it either. I am blessed to teach at a school that allows me to purchase (or download) the books for my students. Many teachers do not have this luxury; they teach what is in the book cabinet.

I also teach *The Glass Menagerie* by Tennessee Williams. I begin the year with this short, powerful play. We read the brilliant essay that Williams wrote titled "The Catastrophe of Success" before we start the play. This essay follows the end of the play in nearly all of the newer editions of the play (at

Williams' insistence). I have students read the essay first. Williams wrote the essay after the production of the first two plays he wrote, *The Glass Menagerie* and *Streetcar Named Desire.* Williams was in his 20s when he wrote these two classic plays. He went from a life of poverty to unimaginable wealth within the span of three years.

I also teach *The Great Gatsby* by F Scott Fitzgerald. *Gatsby* is read by nearly every high school student (though grade levels differ from school to school). One of the great joys of my life has been teaching *The Great Gatsby* to my students. I was not a great fan of *Gatsby* when I started teaching. I knew that it was one of Tim O'Brien's favorite novels; he and I had discussed it during the interview I did with him in the summer of 2004. I did not understand

Fitzgerald's genius until after I started teaching the novel. Having a background on Wall Street helps me teach the nuances of the novel, but it's the prose that makes it magical. I have now read *Gatsby* well over a hundred times. I have taught the novel for ten years now, and I get excited every fall when I get ready to expose my students to the unforgettable characters in the story. In 2013 I took a group of my students to the premier of the movie, starring Leonardo DiCaprio as Gatsby, in Orlando. My students (past and present) were all invited. The theater manager was generous and allowed us to have a 'private screening' in an auditorium all to ourselves. The young men wore tuxedos and nice suits; the girls wore flapper dresses and looked fabulous. We had a great time that night; it was Gatsbyesque (without the

champagne).

My students fall in love with *The Glass Castle*

every spring. Many of them read it once every

year or two after they graduate from high

school. I never dreamed that my students

would love the story the way they do. They can

all relate at some level to Ms. Walls' story.

They love it, and so do I. I love seeing the look

on their faces when I play excerpts from the

interview I did with Jeannette in 2006. They are

not accustomed to hearing the voice of the

author of the books they read. I play the first

five minutes of the interview and they look at

me in amazement. "Is that you talking with

her?" they ask. I tell them it is. By this time of

the school year they have come to understand

that I know a lot of authors, but they have no

frame of reference to place this information in, which makes it fun for me.

In less than a month I will take my new students (and my former students) to see the movie adaptation of *The Glass Castle.* The cast of the film is impressive. Naomi Watts as Rosemary Walls, Woody Harrelson, as Rex Walls, and Brie Larson as the adult Jeannette Walls. One of the challenges of bringing the book to the big screen is the structure of the memoir, which begins when Jeannette was three. The story follows a chronological format (after the two-page opening).

This aspect of the story made casting the film challenging. The director ended up casting three actresses to play Jeannette Walls in the film. Julia Roberts was interested in the book when it was published. Other big names were interested as well (most notably Jennifer Lawrence). I am surprised that it has taken the book over a decade to be produced, and I hope that the time taken to tell the story will be worth the wait. I decided to write this essay prior to the release of the film. I will write a review of the book's adaptation at another time. The list of movies that adequately capture the spirit of a book is relatively short. There is only so much a director can do with 120-150 minutes.

Here is my interview with Jeannette Walls done in early March of 2006:

KK: Jeannette and I met a couple of weeks ago in Jefferson, Texas. I would like to start out by giving a 'shout out' to Kathy Murphy and the

Pulpwood Queens. Kathy just hosted her annual "Pulpwood Queen's Girlfriends Weekend' in Jefferson, Texas, and I had quite a time, and I have a feeling you did too.

JW: Absolutely! It was a great weekend of celebrating reading and of book sharing.

KK: Kathy Murphy is a force of nature; she and her 'girlfriends' do a great job promoting literature. And you also bought a fabulous hat while you were there.

JW: It was an incredible weekend, and it is a fabulous hat!

KK: Jeannette, let's talk about *The Glass Castle*. I read a book from cover to cover, and in your introduction, you dedicate the book to 'John, who convinced me that everyone who is interesting has a past.' I really like that. I come from an alcoholic family as well, but you transcend the reality of an alcoholic family and show that we all come from some kind of past- and I like the way you opened the book that way. There is a universal truth that the book captures.

JW: My husband really did pull the story out of me, Kacey. For years and years, I hid my past and tried to run away from it, running away from who I really was. I was living in New York City, a reporter covering high-society and celebrities, and I lived in fear of people finding out who I really was. My husband eventually found out about my past after I married him,

31

and he basically duck-taped me to my desk and said 'You're writing this. You're going to write it as a book and you're telling everything.' And I truly believed that after *The Glass Castle* was published that I would lose my job, lose my friends, and lose whatever meager standing in society that I had. And, Kacey, I have never been more wrong about anything in my life.

First of all, I completely underestimated people's capacity for compassion, to really understand a story. But, more importantly, I completely underestimated the degree to which everyone out there does have a story, whether they came from a hardscrabble background like I did, or whether they went off to boarding schools and live on Park Avenue. Everyone has something they believe makes them different, or inferior, or weird, and I think, very often, that's the best thing you have going for you. And it's taken me this long to figure that out.

****

I always pause the interview at this point and ask my students what they think of what she just said. I repeat the critical quote *"everyone has something that makes them feel different, or inferior, or weird, and I think, very often, that's the best thing you have going for you."* This statement is profound for a teenager to hear. Jeannette Walls is telling them that it's okay to not fit in; that the very thing that makes them unpopular at school is what will lead them to success in the world. The young girl who dresses oddly and secretly wants to be a fashion designer suddenly has an ally in Jeannette Walls. The young boy who everyone thinks has it made (yet in reality comes to school hungry most days) suddenly feels hope. This gift of giving the hopeless hope is what makes *The Glass Castle* so remarkable. I see lives changed by this book every year. This is the power of literature in a young person's life.

****

KK: I agree with you. I come from an alcoholic family, my father drank himself to death when he was 46 years old, I was nineteen years old at the time. As I was reading *The Glass Castle,* some of the scenes felt like they were taken from my own home, and I think that for those of us who come from alcoholic homes the memoir is very familiar, we've gone through similar things. Yet someone who does not understand alcoholism might think that your story could not have actually happened.

JW: (laughing) That's actually happened to me a number of times. I've had people say, 'I can't believe you've lived through all of this', I've had people say they can't believe my father was an alcoholic, that he was as articulate and creative as I say he was in the book. And to those people I say, 'Honey, you need to do a little bit of research, or maybe do some volunteer work. Because alcoholics can be charming, beguiling, and manipulative; and my father was. Yet I don't depict him as being a bad guy, because I don't believe he was- he was a flawed human being. And some people have told me that what resonated with them in the story was that I didn't vilify my parents. My father was not a bad guy, my mother was not an alcoholic; she was a little loopy, but she was a good person. And while there was chaos and depravation at times, there was also a lot of love and intelligence. And I just think it's important for everyone to focus on what's good in your life, and not always dwell on the bad.

We moved around a lot when I was growing up, we lived in more towns than I could count by the time that I was ten. Then when I was 10 we moved to a town in West Virginia that didn't have indoor plumbing, and we often went without food; but on the upside, my parents always put an emphasis on learning and reading, and I really do believe my parents loved me, and I do believe it's important to learn from the bad, but also to cherish the good, because to every upside there's a downside, and to try to learn from that.

KK: Absolutely. When I re-read the book preparing for our interview a couple of things jumped out at me, and really resonated with me. My father was my hero, and I understand the image of the 'glass castle' very well. On page 38 [paperback edition] you wanted to pull out the sapling of a Joshua Tree and replant it, and your mother frowned and said that you would be destroying what makes the Joshua Tree special, that it was the Joshua Tree's struggle that gave it it's beauty.

JW: I love it that you zeroed in on that passage, because that happens to be one of my favorite passages that not a lot of critics have zeroed in on, and I think that is almost at the heart of the book. My parents both loved challenges, and they believed that life shouldn't be easy, and that it was these difficulties that you learned from. They were suspicious of 'cushy lives'- I think they went a bit overboard on that- but they truly believed that you learned from these hardships, and that children should not be coddled, and it's something that my mother believes very much to this day.

KK: Then on page 56 you write a scene where your family is spread out on the floor reading a dictionary and if you disagreed with a letter that you would write a letter to the publisher, debating their use of the word. And, once again, I think that it blows most people's minds to think of an alcoholic family doing that, but when I was growing up if I didn't know how to spell a word, I had to look it up, write it down, and use it in a sentence.

LW: You're kidding me! I love hearing that, because that was such a constant scene in my family; looking words up and discussing different meanings words had. And I've had so many people that are shocked by that. They say, 'but I thought your father was a drunk!' And I say, 'Yes, he was a drunk, but he was an intelligent drunk.'

Some people who have read *The Glass Castle* see my father as this belligerent loser and see my mother as the world's worst mother that ever existed, and they think my parents should have been locked up and put in jail, and yet others see the good in them. I think it's almost a litmus test that you come to the story with, but yes, it's a very, very vivid memory for me.

KK: *The Glass Castle* also deals with the dark side of the alcoholic family, and there are several scenes that border on being abusive. When I read the scene about you being in the bar when you were a teenager I became very uncomfortable, I could relate to that tension in the story. In the world we live in today, there probably would have been an intervention, but that was not the case when we were growing up.

JW: You're right. You're very smart, you're zeroing in on many of the pivotal passages. That summer, when I was 13, was very significant for me, because I finally had to face the truth about my father. There's no doubt that he loved me, but when I sat down and thought about it, he needed and loved alcohol more. It was the toughest scene for me to write, because I still loved my father, and I felt like I was betraying him; but at the same time, if I had not written that scene I would have been betraying the truth.

I do believe there's an upside to every downside, and the upside was that it showed me loud and clear that I had to get out. I realized my father was not going to protect me and the only one going to save me was myself. If my father had behaved himself just a little more I might have stayed at home and tried to make things work.

But it was that summer that I started saving money to go to New York City.

KK: That same summer you had a conflict with your mother. You had been holding the family together and when an important event happens your father backs your mother and whips you. And something snapped inside you. I was right there with you when I read that scene because I have been there myself.

JW: That was the first time I can remember speaking to my parents that way- saying 'you guys are wrong'. As wacky as my family was, in many ways we were very traditional, and mom and dad were head of the household, and I sort of bought into that structure.

That summer I was bringing in the only paycheck, and I was still expected to obey the rules of the household, and you're right, something inside me snapped and I thought, 'this is wrong', this is not going to work, and I cannot make it work.

There was no doubt in my mind that summer, that when mom went away for awhile, that I could straighten my father out, that what he really needed was a strong woman who would set rules and make him live by them. I thought that at age 13 I was strong enough to do that and I wasn't, and it made me 'wake up and smell the coffee honey.'

KK: It literally broke my heart when your father stole the 'Oz fund' that you and your sister had. When I read that scene, it was just devastating.

JW: For your listeners, what happened was we put all of our savings into this big, pink, piggy bank that we were going to use as an escape fund to go to New York City, and one reader told me that when she was reading that scene she was yelling, 'Don't put that money in the piggy bank!!'

It occurred to me that maybe I should hide the money, but I thought that since my brother, my sister, and I were all contributing to it that if we tried to hide it dad would find it anyway, so I thought that since it was out in the open that not even dad would steal it, but I was wrong, and he did. He stole the money.

KK: You know, Jeannette, what I think that shows you is that you are not an alcoholic, but he was.

JW: Yes, that's true. But it also showed me that I just simply had to get out; just find a way to

get out, and we did. It did break my heart a
little, I had to stop believing in him and believe
in myself instead.

KK: And you even said, 'Dad, go ahead and
build your 'glass castle', but don't do it for me.

JW: Yes, I did. Dad was always talking about
building us this 'glass castle' that would be
solar-powered and be built entirely from glass,
and whenever times got really tough dad would
pull his blueprints of the 'glass castle' out and
that summer I finally came to realize that the
'glass castle' was never going to be built, at
least not for me.
   But, in a way, some people have accused me
of being fatalistically optimistic, even though
the physical structure of the 'glass castle' was

never built, dad did give us dreams, and a

hope for the future. That's why I named the

book *The Glass Castle,* because even though

we weren't given the physical building, we

were given hopes and dreams, and in the long

run I think those are more important.

   Ideally you get both, but in the long run I

think nurturing the heart, the soul, and the

head are more important than the stomach.

KK: I agree, though it took me many years to

understand that. Looking back now I can see

that the values my father instilled in me have

been more valuable than money would have

been at the time. I think of your story about

Chuck Yeager when we talk about these

things. That sounded like a life-changing

experience for you. Here you are living in a

small town in West Virginia, and Chuck Yeager comes to visit your school. You were ready for Chuck Yeager!

JW: Absolutely! You know, Kacey, so much about life is how you perceive it. It sounds to me like you had a childhood where you could have focused on the negative, you could have felt sorry for yourself, so it really is a choice on how you choose to see these things.

When Chuck Yeager came to town he was my father's personal hero, and he stayed up with me all night so that I would have intelligent questions to ask him. Mr. Yeager was the first person to ever travel faster than the speed of sound, and my father made sure that I was prepared to take advantage of this opportunity.

I came to New York when I was 17 years old, I hadn't even finished high school, and people ask me, 'How did you possibly make it? and the truth is that the hard-scrabble way of life that I had growing up did prepare me for what was to come, and both of my parents, particularly my father, constantly encouraged me and supported my dreams.

One of the many lies that my father told me (and I believed him) was that I could do anything I put my mind to. And I believed him. If I'd have been a little more intelligent I might not have believed him, but that belief got me through some tough times.

KK: So eventually you, and all of your siblings, moved to New York. I must admit that I laughed out loud when you wrote about when your parents decided to move to New York to be with all of you. Tell us how that happened.

JW: I'm getting ready for school and there is a traffic report on, and a van had broken down on FDR Drive and the contents had spilled out all over the street, and a dog was loose. It was a mess, and the DJs were having a big chuckle about the whole thing, but my heart really sunk for the people in the van, because that kind of thing happened to me all the time when I was growing up. But I didn't think a whole lot more of it until later that afternoon I got a call, and it was my mother and she said, 'Jeanettie-kins', we've moved to New York', and all of the sudden my heart seized up and I said 'Mom, did your van break down on the FDR this morning? 'and she said, 'How did you know?'

So, I told her I heard about it on the radio and she took that as a really good sign, because they had just moved to New York and already they were famous.

KK: From that point on the book becomes about how the members of your family chose (or chose not to) become involved with what was actually your parent's choice of lifestyle. And, not to give too much away, but you learn (towards the end of the book) of some significant assets that that your mother has that must have blown your mind.

JW: Exactly. One of the conclusions I've come to is that it was my parent's choice to live the way they did. And I also believe that many people have the lives that they want, that they have chosen for themselves. I do believe my parents could have changed their lives if they had wanted to.

A lot of people ask me if I'm angry with my parents because they hadn't changed their lifestyle. For my part, I am very happy with where I am in my life. My parents could have changed their lives. People ask me, 'what did you do with your anger?' The truth is I have a fabulous job, and a great life, there is no reason for me to be angry. It doesn't matter how you got where you are, what's important is that you got there.

The truth is I could have had a much more conventional life had my parents chose to live differently. They were completely capable of it. My mother is very intelligent, and my father is a very smart man. But they did choose this crazy life- my mother describes herself as 'an excitement addict'. As far as I'm concerned, it's okay, you learn a lot from your hardships.

Before I came out of the closet about my past I had a very well to do friend who wanted me to take an "Outward Bound" expedition with her. I had never heard of "Outward Bound." She described it as this incredible experience where you go out into the wilderness and you survive on your own, and I'm thinking 'this sounds like the first 17 years of my life.' It was the funniest thing I'd ever heard. Rich people paying to have this kind of experience! Then, after I thought about it, it made sense.

Everything in life had been given to this lady on a silver platter, and inside she had this gnawing doubt of whether she could do it or not. There was no doubt in my mind whether she could do it or not, she was very capable and very intelligent. But she didn't know that.

So, if you have a life where you've earned everything you have, there's a certain comfort in that, a certain sense of self that comes with that. But it's your choice; you have to decide how you want to live.

KK: Jeannette, I'm at a point in my life, I'm 48 now, where I almost feel sorry for people that had a normal childhood.

JW: (laughing) I'm with you on that. They certainly have a difficult time digging up the goods for a memoir!

KK: The photographer, Diane Arbus, took pictures of what she called "freaks". She got to know them and then took their picture. She said that, 'freaks were the true aristocrats in life; that most people are born and live their lives trying to avoid trauma. Freaks are born into this life with with trauma, so they understand life right away, where most people never truly understand life until they face trauma for the first time.'

JW: Wow. I love that, it's very intelligent. I think that's true. If you grow up and your childhood is too easy, then you think that life will be easy. It's interesting; a number of psychiatrists are saying that parents who try to give their children lives that are 'trauma-free' are doing them a huge disservice. I'm not enough of an expert to know whether that's true or not, but a number of people have asked me how they can provide for their children, but not be overly protective of them, and I don't really know the answer to that.

I do think that as a society we have so much materially that I hope we don't take things for granted. I grew up without indoor plumbing, so I know that I will never take certain things for granted, a hot bath for example. Or even a flush toilet, these things are incredible luxuries.

KK: I agree. Jeannette, the last part of *The Glass Castle* is titled "Homecoming". It describes your life with your husband, John, and you give the readers an update on your family. It's like a snapshot. When you wrote the first draft, was this ending the one you had in mind? It is relatively short, but it is very powerful.

JW: Yes, it was. The first part and the fifth part are both short. Originally the part that was much longer was the part in New York. Part One is seeing my mother on the street, part two is the desert, part three is our time in West Virginia, and part four is about my time in New York. Originally part four was much longer, I described New York society and wrote about the people that lived on Park Avenue, that even though their lives looked perfect from a distance, in fact they did not have the answers to finding happiness. It's such a cliché that 'money can't buy happiness', and I knew that was true. But I grew up poor, so I believed that having money would make life easier.

It was shocking to see the degree that that these people that had such wealth were constantly suing their siblings or not talking to their parents. I ended up cutting that part of the book out because it felt churlish and read like "The Nanny Diaries Revisited".

So, part five ended up being the length I originally thought it would be.

KK: I loved the intimacy you showed in part five. There is a misconception that people from 'dysfunctional families' are incapable of having healthy relationships. And you disprove that with part five.

JW: I think we treasure it even more! When you see stability, and happiness, and someone who understands you, you say, 'this is so great!' I am very happily married now, and I have so much to be grateful for; that's why I ended the book with "Thanksgiving". To have a house, to have food on the table, to be with those I love, is really a blessing. There is so much to be thankful for.

KK: Well said. Jeannette, before we end I would like to mention the 'hot topic' of the literary world right now. In fact, you and I discussed this when we were in Texas. I don't want to wander too far into it, but I would like to discuss James Frey's memoir "A Million Little Pieces."

If you study ancient Greek storytelling, you have logos, ethos, and pathos. Pathos is the idea of sympathetic pity. As I was reading *The Glass Castle* I realized that you experienced a lot of painful things in your life, and you didn't have to make them up. You relied on your memory and your imagination to write the book. You can't have fact-checkers looking at every detail of your life. I know it's a tough question, but what is your take on the controversy?

JW: I think memoir writing is all about honesty. It's about the truth: not just factual truth, but emotional truth as well. And it's very hard to get at. The first draft of *the Glass Castle* was too emotionally distant from what really happened. It took me about six weeks to write the first version. Then I spent about five years to get at the truth. Did it really happen this way? Could it have actually happened that way? You can't do fact checking, that's not what memoir is about. I bounced things off of my family. My brother, Brian, who has an incredible memory, was a great help. It is a matter of what happened and how did you really feel about it. When memoir is successful you're sharing your experience; you're saying this is who I am, and this is what I went through. You can take the reader on that journey, the journey of your life. If you're successful you can help the reader learn something from your life.

But if it's not honest, on the most profound level, if you're not painfully honest with yourself and with your reader, then there's just no point in it. This has been one of the most incredible gratifying things about writing the book- while I was writing it I was thinking about how strange and how bizarre my story was- in order for a memoir to work something has to be universal, and as I wrote I thought what is universal about this wacky family? How could people possibly relate to it? But the stunning thing has been how universal my story is; that people like you can relate to it.

You seem like a perfectly normal person (we both laugh), and you seized on to the story because similar things happened to you, so you know it's true. In the isolation of my own shame, I thought I was the only one who had ever gone through this. It feels like *Alice Through the Looking Glass* in reverse, looking through the looking glass backwards and finding all of these wonderful people that I can relate to. Many readers have corresponded with me telling me they have gone through similar things. And the thought of violating this truth offends me terribly. I could never have made this stuff up; the idea of throwing four kids into the back of a U-Haul never would have occurred to me! What was important was to understand why all of these happened and to make sense of them. To lie about the basic fundamental truth seems to be not only dishonest, but potentially dangerous, because you're leading people with a distorted map of life and I think that's dangerous.

KK: I agree completely. I hope we don't go too far the other way now because of Frey's book. There's an implicit trust between readers and writers that is very important.

JW: Very well said.

KK: Jeannette, thank you for taking so much time out of what I know is a busy schedule.

JW: You're welcome, Kacey. It's been an honor.

****

One of the beautiful things about my life is what I have learned from reading books. I discovered their magic 55 years ago, and my love of the printed word has never diminished, it has continued to grow. I love the word serendipity. This word defines my literary life.

I started a website in 2004 to help readers and authors connect with each other. At that point in my life I had lost the 'fear' of meeting writers. I came to realize that they were people like me who loved books- they loved them so much they spent their free time writing them. Many writers are shy and love the isolation that writing affords them. They prefer to sit in their writing rooms and write beautiful stories versus driving all across the country promoting their work.

That is why people like Kathy Murphy and I exist, we bring readers and writers together to get to know each other. Serendipity. In January 2006 my life was going smoothly, and I thought I knew what the next decade would bring. I was wrong. I changed jobs, got divorced, moved to a new state, and started over. I became an English teacher, a job I absolutely love. I get to share my love of reading and writing with teenagers. I kept my website alive and became friends with my literary heroes. That's where this new series "A Celebration of Words" was created.

I was doing my first interview in June 2004 with Andre Dubus III to kick-off my website, The

Kacey Kowars Show. I clearly remember how nervous I was. I thought "who am I to interview Andre Dubus, Tim O'Brien, and Nelson DeMille?" I called Andre on the phone to do my first interview. We chatted about his father and then I started the tape rolling. "Welcome to The Kacey Kowars Show, a celebration of words." I have no idea where that tag line "a celebration of words" came from. It was just there. I can assure you that I never dreamed that 13 years later I would begin writing a series of books about the authors I met and interviewed along my journey. My reality has exceeded my dreams.

To bring this essay full-circle: Kathy Murphy and I have remained close friends. She has gone through her own journey since we met in 2005. I recently finished my first book and sent her a copy. She invited me to the 2018 Pulpwood Queens' Bohemian Rhapsody Girlfriends Weekend in January. The celebration was held in Nacogdoches, Texas. My wife, Sharon, and I attended. I spoke on one of the panels and Kathy selected my book as one her recommended books for 2018. It was a thrill to be among the hundreds of booklovers that took over the town in January. Alice Hoffman, one of the keynote speakers, delivered a moving speech. I interviewed Ms. Hoffman in 2006. Lisa Wingate was the other keynote speaker. Her book *Before They Were Yours* recently passed a million copies in sales. Ms. Wingate has been a regular speaker at The Pulpwood Queens weekend.

Who knows, maybe the next Jeannette Walls will be attending the 2019 Girlfriends

Weekend? But it is not the fame and fortune that matters. It is the magic that happens when like-minded people get together and talk about books. Serendipity.

I look forward to heading back to Nacogdoches in January 2019 for another world-class weekend of book sharing.

Part Two

Dreams Do Come True

James Lee Burke

Dreams do come true. I moved to Indianapolis in 1986 to open a new office for a regional stock brokerage firm, The Ohio Company. I was 29 years old. I picked up a copy of *The Neon Rain*, the first book in a new series written by an author named James Lee Burke. I had never heard of Mr. Burke. The dust jacket caught my attention. It was black, and the 'neon' colors that cut across the front of the jacket caught my eye. I picked up the book and read the blurbs on the back of the dust jacket. I can still see the book and the bookstore in my mind's eye. I was standing in a Barnes & Noble at the Castleton Mall. The bookstore was crowded. This was before bookstores had coffee shops inside. I drove past two other bookstores to come to this particular location because I liked the selection they carried. *The Neon Rain* was on the "New Books" table.

I bought the book and began reading it that night. I had begun reading in earnest three years before, when I stopped drinking. I now had more time on my hands and developed a love affair with the modern American mystery that continues to this day. I was beginning to understand the craft of writing at a more advanced level than I had in the past. I had started my own attempt at writing a mystery, but I was too busy with my brokerage career to spend much time at it. Besides, I had already read enough to know that I had a long way to go before what I wrote would be publishable.

James Lee Burke, and his character, Dave Robicheaux, changed the trajectory of my life, just as Andre Dubus had three years earlier.

His style, and his command of language, captivated me. Robicheaux was a recovering alcoholic; he went to meetings, struggled with his character defects, and had a moral compass that I admired. I read the book in two or three days, and then I read it again. Burke took great risks with his writing (he wrote about evil men and women in a frighteningly real manner). The characters in the novel were richly drawn and morally complex.

The following year I was in that same bookstore when I saw Burke's second Robicheaux novel, *Heaven's Prisoners*. I bought the book and raced home, ready to immerse myself in Robicheaux's world again. The depth of the characters and the quality of the prose were even stronger in the second book. There was an image in the story that has haunted me for nearly 30 years. There is a young girl being walked to her death at a concentration camp in Germany. Her sock slips down into her shoe, and as she reaches down to pull it up, Burke writes "the innocent who suffer for the rest of us become anointed and loved by God in a special way; the votive candle of their lives had made them heaven's prisoners." The sentence brought tears to my eyes; the imagery and the passion of the scene were so vivid to me. I would never had dreamed that day that Mr. Burke and I would discuss that very sentence 20 years later (and that he had the photograph of the girl framed in his office).

The next year saw the publication of *Black Cherry Blues,* and another Edgar Award for best mystery novel. I felt a kinship with Mr.

Burke. We were fellow travelers on life's journey; we experienced things in a similar fashion. It was more than the recovery from alcoholism, much more.

Burke's work appeals to all five senses. You can smell the pecan trees and feel the mist coming off of the rivers where he fishes. You can hear the sound of the insects that speak to Robicheaux during his sleepless nights. You can taste the sandwiches that Clete Purcel (perhaps the greatest sidekick since Watson) devours. You visualize the touch that Robicheaux feels when he makes love to his wife, Bootsie.

There are certainly other great mystery writers who use literary style and technique to add richness to their prose. But James Lee Burke began distancing himself from other writers with *The Neon Rain*. Raymond Chandler moved the needle on the mystery novel in the 1940s and 1950s. His character, Philip Marlowe, took the pulp-fiction genre and created an art form out of it. Chandler was a brilliant, educated man, who wrote about societies (particularly Los Angeles's) ills using the mystery novel as his canvas.

Other mystery writers helped shape the direction of the genre as well. Ross MacDonald created the Lew Archer series. MacDonald wrote intricate mysteries that integrated family backgrounds and the dangers of keeping secrets into an art form. Paul Newman played Archer in a film titled HARPER that created a growing audience for MacDonald's work.

John D McDonald created the beloved character, Travis McGee. McDonald's series took place in Fort Lauderdale, and his sidekick was an economist named Meyer. Together they solved problems and unraveled mysteries. The stories were both entertaining and enlightening. Travis McGee helped women in distress. He preferred a solitary life, and most of his relationships were transitory, but he treated women well, and stayed in touch with them after their crisis had passed.

The majority of the great mystery series characters that 'walked the mean streets' of their cities led solitary lives. One of the elements that make Dave Robicheaux different, and more fully developed, is his commitment to marriage; the effort he puts into his relationships with the women in his life. He listens to the women in his life- he intuitively knows that the women that love him see a part of him that he is incapable of seeing. It is in Robicheaux's nature to defend the innocent, the naive, the underdog, and the segment of the human population that has been on the wrong side of history. At times Robicheaux acts like a violent priest, dispensing justice in a manner that the Pope might not approve of. He is willing to live with the consequences of taking the law into his own hands (when necessary).

When I begin a new James Lee Burke novel I know I will stop often to do research on historical events and biblical stories that he places in his novels for a very precise purpose. Burke's knowledge of the history of gangsters, the blues, the Bible, and world history is encyclopedic. As I mature as a reader I

continue to admire the specific details Burke
uses in his novels.

I have had the honor of becoming friends
with Mr. Burke. I have interviewed him ten
times on my website and have exchanged
postcards and emails with him for over 20
years.

In 1992 I wrote Mr. Burke a letter, the second
such letter I had written to an author: the first
being the one I sent to his cousin, Andre
Dubus, in 1984. I was living in Indianapolis at
the time, still managing the regional brokerage
firm. Never in my wildest dreams did I imagine
that I would ever leave the career I was
working in, or that my love of reading would
develop into a passion that I continue to pursue
to this day. I simply wanted to tell him how
much I enjoyed his first three novels and

thanked him for writing them. I also included some personal information about my life, and some of the similar roads we had trudged together. I also told him of my friendship with his cousin, Andre Dubus. After discovering the Robicheaux series I soon learned that Burke had published six books between the years 1965-1986.

In fact, *The Lost Get Back Boogie*, published by LSU Press in 1986, had been a finalist for The Pulitzer Prize. His first novel, *Half of Paradise*, was published in 1965, when Burke was in his 20s. For a span of 13 years, Burke's work appeared in paperback editions, rather than hardcover. In fact, *The Lost Get Back Boogie,* was rejected 121 times before finding a publisher, a number that Burke believes to be a record.

In my first letter I asked him about this 13-year span of time. In the first postcard he sent me he wrote:

"Dear Kacey, thank you for your thoughtful letter and all of your kind remarks about my work. I appreciate your comments very much. You're surely right about Andre: he's a great writer, maybe the best short story writer in America. My wife and I start a tour this month which takes us to Boston and I hope Andre and I will be able to do a signing together. I can't say exactly why I couldn't publish in hardback for those 13 years, but today I adhere to the notion that if a guy just keeps hanging around, he finally gets back in fashion. Anyway, thanks again for all your good words, and please excuse this rushed note, but I'm running a little behind in everything and next week we start a

20-city tour that will take us away from home for about five weeks or so. Anyway, I hope to meet you sometime. Meanwhile, I appreciate your kindness very much.

Your friend,

Jim Burke

   The postcard was sent from Missoula, Montana, and had his home address on it. The cover was a gorgeous picture of Rock Creek. I was touched the day I received it, and I am touched all these years later, that Burke shared his home address with me. The postcard was actually typed out on a manual typewriter.

   It had been eight years since my first correspondence with Andre Dubus in 1984. I was beginning to understand at a deeper level that God had given me a gift when I was born. I have an unnatural attraction to books. I always have, and I think it's safe to say (at the age of 61) that I always will have this feeling towards words, sentences, paragraphs, and chapters. I was still twelve years away from the idea of my website, and 15 years away from beginning my second career as a high school English teacher.

I remember vividly my first year in the classroom. The year was 2007, and I had a brilliant young woman in my class that absorbed everything I said like a sponge. Her writing improved dramatically as she discovered the link between critical reading and writing. One day after school she stopped by my classroom. "Mr. Kowars, can I ask you a question?"

"Sure", I said.

"How many books have you read in your lifetime?" she asked. It was a good question.

"I need a more specific time frame", I told her.

"Since you got out of college," she said.

"Let me think for a minute," I said. "I quit drinking in 1984, and I started my website in 2004. During that time I read, on average, two novels a week. So, I'll say the number is around 2,000."

Her jaw dropped. She was genuinely dumbfounded. I was surprised by her reaction. I knew I read a lot but had never really put a number to it.

I then remembered an event that took place in the mid-90s when working for The Ohio Company. The president of the company, Don Fanta, was a good friend of mine. He was a mentor to me at this time of my life. He did not drink, and he read voraciously.

"I'll tell you a story I just remembered," I told Kaley. "I was at a national sales conference in Columbus, Ohio, sitting next to the president of the company. The motivational speaker that day was listing the common traits of successful people. He began talking about reading. Don Fanta, the president of the company, and I were sitting next to each other in the front row. There were probably thirty rows of seats behind us.

"The speaker stopped and said, 'How many of you here today read a book last year? How many of you read between 2-5 books last year? How about 6-12?"

I told Kaley that Don and I were raising our hands and not really paying attention to what everyone else was doing.

"How many of you read 25 books last year?"

Once again Don and I stuck our hands up, but now the speaker was focusing his gaze on the two of us.

"How about 50?"

Don looked at me, and I looked at him. I raised my hand, Don did not.

The speaker asked me how many books I read in the previous year. I said, "I'll guess between 75-100."

"Just so you know," the speaker said, "you two were the only ones that kept raising your hands after I got past 12." Laughter broke out behind us.

Kaley laughed when I told her this story. I told her that some of the other salespeople thought I was exaggerating, but I wasn't. I had forgotten that incident, but it must have occurred around the time I began corresponding with James Lee Burke.

Kaley was pleased with my answers, and left my classroom telling me that once she got out of college she was going to read as many novels as she possibly could. I am happy to report that Kaley is still reading, pursuing her passions in life, and now writing songs. Her first collection of songs was released in 2017.

The next letter I wrote to Mr. Burke was in 1993, after reading *In the Electric Mist With Confederate Dead*, one of my favorite

Robicheaux novels. I mentioned my admiration of Robert Sims Reid's *Big Sky*, a wonderful mystery set in Montana. Montana is home to many of our country's finest writers.

A few weeks later I received another typed postcard from Montana:

Dear Kacey, thanks for your fine letter. In fact, you write awfully well yourself. Anyway, I appreciate very much all your kind remarks about my work. They're truly touching and mean a lot to me. I'll also pass on your good words to Bob Reid when I see him. By the way, he's a fine guy. I'm glad you like *Electric Mist* so much. I'm real proud of it; Time, People, and Entertainment Weekly are coming out with pretty good spreads in the next couple of weeks. *Mist* looks to be a winner. Thanks again for all your kind words. Pearl and I start a 21-city tour April 18. I'm getting over the hill for all this stuff.

All the best, your pal

Jim Burke

In 1995 I moved back to Columbus, Ohio and went to work with a friend of mine who owned his own stock brokerage business. I continued working and reading. The idea of teaching writing, reviewing books, or interviewing authors was still a decade away. The stock market was doing well, I was making plenty of money, and my world was good.

I expanded my collection of rare first editions. I miss the days of flying to New York and browsing through used bookstores, finding rare first editions on the shelves like buried treasures. I miss going to The Strand and visiting their rare book collection. I miss Hoffman's Bookstore on the campus of Ohio State University; a place I could go and spend hours combing the shelves looking for the one book that would complete a section of my collection. Video killed the radio song. The internet killed the book store.

One day, in New York, I came across a rare limited edition of one of Andre Dubus' short stories. It was bound in leather, numbered, and signed by Dubus. I put it on my bookshelf and there is sat for two years. I finished one of Burke's novels in 1998, and on a whim, I sent the Dubus book to Burke in Missoula for a Christmas present. Time passed, and I did not hear from Burke, but I was not expecting a prompt reply.

Dreams do come true- but in my life they have not come true on my time-table- and that is a good thing. My ambitions have changed over the nearly 60 years I have walked this earth. In my twenties, thirties, and forties, my goals were materialistic; and that is natural. I wanted a great job, a family, good health, and to help others when it was convenient. From the ages of 27-48, I largely achieved my goals. I have always been hardworking and ambitious.

In 1999, I was 42 years old. The stock market was doing well, and I was content with my life. I was working from home one beautiful spring morning. My dog, a beagle named Karma, sat beside my desk on the days I worked from home. When she needed to go outside, she walked to the door and barked. On that morning I answered her call and took her for a long walk, enjoying the warm weather, while Karma sniffed her usual places.

After 30 minutes we returned home, and I saw a blinking red light on my answering machine. This was during the pre-cellular days when answering machines were considered high-tech. I looked at the number on the machine and it read 'caller-ID blocked'. That meant that the call had probably come from a phone solicitor. I pushed the playback button and heard the following message: "Hey there partner, it's Jim Burke calling. I want to thank you for your beautiful gift and let you know that I was in New Iberia over the holidays and just returned. I have never seen this copy and I will treasure it. I hope our paths cross down the line. Over and out."

I felt like I had been punched in the stomach. I hit #69 on my phone (which automatically redialed the previous call). I looked at Karma, angry that she had chosen that moment for her walk. I listened to the message again, hoping that Burke had left his phone number, but he had not.

The magnitude of my discomfort did not make sense to me. After all, James Lee Burke is just a writer. But something changed inside of me that day, and I felt another call towards leaving the business world for the world of literature, but I had absolutely no idea how I could do that. It was inconceivable. I had a wife and a step-daughter, and I loved what I did for a living. I played golf at a country club, had a generous expense account, travelled the world, and had most of the creature comforts I could imagine. How could I ever make a living writing books; let alone reading them?

On that day in 1999 I would never have believed that in July 2005 I would have a website where I did live interviews with authors; and that I would do the first of ten live interviews with James Lee Burke. The idea that I would have Mr. Burke's contact information in both New Iberia, Louisiana, and Missoula, Montana, would have been beyond my wildest dreams. Inconceivable. But all of that happened- and much, much more.

Mr. Burke and I hit it off during our first 45-minute interview. We began exchanging emails a couple of times a year, and I became part of his publishing cycle. I came to know his daughter, Pamala, who runs his website, and interviewed his daughter, Alafair, in 2011. Each time I interviewed him Pamala would feature the interview on the home page of his website (in fact they are all still there). The interviews I have done with Burke have generated more emails to my website than the interviews I have down with any other author. His fan base is well educated, loyal, and are excellent readers. I have received emails from all over the world thanking me for the interviews.

Writing this essay in the year 2018, I can only attribute the rest of this essay describing my ongoing relationship with James Lee Burke as a gift from God. I began this journey after 9/11. The world changed on September 11, 2001, and it has never been the same; nor have I. The world experienced a change like that of the characters in *The Great Gatsby*. I have been teaching *Gatsby* in my classroom for ten years now, and its moral lessons are eternal; still relevant today.

KK: Jim, you and I discussed your wonderful book of short stories, *Jesus Out to Sea,* a few weeks ago. The title story involves Father Jude LeBlanc, a priest who serves a parish in New Orleans. He believes that Hurricane Katrina was not the result of bombs being set off in the ninth ward; he offers a different perspective. Could you explain that reference?

JLB: When the storm hit, people were terrified. The people in the ninth ward said they heard explosions, and they feared that terrorists, or racists, were dynamiting the levees. And Dave Robicheaux said, 'No terrorists were needed, the levee began to come apart.'

The lower ninth ward was inundated with water and many died.

KK: On page 34 of *The Tin Roof Blowdown* [hardcover edition], you explained that within one night the entire city of New Orleans was, technologically speaking, taken back to the Middle Ages. It affected everyone.

JLB: That's right. All of us have experienced this to one extent or another, say, for example, 'brownouts'. But in this instance, as Dave says, the entire power grid of the city was made null and void, and this 21st century city metropolis, was suddenly just like a Medieval city in Europe in the year 1300.

KK: One of the things I liked about this novel is the development of Dave Robicheaux's character, his maturity at being able to better understand the things he can change in his life. He says that, 'the truth is I don't want to talk about it. If age brings wisdom, it lies in the realization that most talk is useless, and you stay out of other people's grief.'

That seems like a big change to me, Jim, because in the past he might have gone off on some tangents. He keeps his eye on the ball pretty well in *The Tin Roof Blowdown.*

JLB: He makes that statement on two levels. One is the fact that rhetoric really solved no problem, and ultimately the only thing that thwarts evil is the application of good against it. But when he cautions himself in not involving himself in other people's grief, he often doesn't take his own advice. I think that tension, that ethical tension, is what afflicts all of us to some degree.

We have to become involved in the lives of others. We have to help those in need. But at the same time, we have to be able to choose our battle grounds with some degree of wisdom. There's no formula that always works.

KK: Exactly. We all knew that there was looting going on in New Orleans after Katrina. But part of the beauty of the novel's plot is the

97

retribution that happens when some gang members pick on the wrong guy to prey upon. They take some things they will regret stealing.

JLB: Yes, these looters, and there were several of them, are supposedly under the command of Bertrand Melancon. These guys were professional wise guys, gang bangers, street pukes; there are lots of names for them, but they've stolen a boat, a power boat and they're looting homes in the uptown section of New Orleans, and they choose an abandoned home that is filled with all sorts of interesting things. They rip the walls out and fill pillow cases with jewelry, cocaine, and counterfeit money they stumble upon. And then, after they're done, they decide to vandalize the place.

Dave Robicheaux says that 'it looked like an army of Visigoths had invaded this antebellum home.' They used garden rakes to tear chandeliers out of the ceiling, they urinate in the refrigerator's seasoning drawer: it's incredible what these guys do. They destroy the interior of the home, not knowing that the home belongs to Sidney Kovick, the most dangerous gangster in New Orleans- a guy who might have cut off another man's legs with a chainsaw. When they discover whose home, they've robbed and vandalized they're terrified.

KK: And rightly so.

JLB: Sidney Kovick is not a nice guy, he's very dangerous. In fact, Clete Purcel once bounced Kovick's head up-and-down on a concrete slab when he was a kid, and Kovic has never

forgotten who did that to him.

KK: Clete is back and in fine form in *The Tin Roof Blowdown,* and we know that Clete is not going to evacuate. He's not the kind of guy who leaves when the authorities announce that things have gotten dangerous. Anywhere Clete is at is dangerous.

JLB: Right. Clete's a great character. We meet him in the first pages of the book, when he is in the [French] quarter just as Katrina is making landfall in New Orleans.

KK: I also liked the character Otis in this book. He and Dave have great conversations about the nature of the father-daughter bond, about the bond's strength.

JLB: Otis Baylor is one of my favorite characters, not just in this book, but in any that I've written. He's an insurance salesman from north Alabama, whose father and uncle had both been members of the Klu Klux Klan. But he's cut out of different cloth, he's a very decent man, and he's radicalized politically by what he sees being done to many people whose claims are being unfairly denied by insurance companies.

KK: We discussed *Pegasus Descending* over a year ago, Jim. At that time, we talked about the confluence of events that took place in order for Dave Robicheaux to be the 'narrator' of this ongoing story. Some of the things we talked about then are becoming more visible today [2006]. The depth and the magnitude of the fraud and the cover-up are becoming more apparent every day.

Against this backdrop of corruption Otis Baylor begins to realize a part of himself that even he is afraid of.

LLN: He discovers that he has a far greater potential for violence than he thought. And his daughter, of course, is a victim of a gang rape. She is raped by these same men that have been robbing and vandalizing the homes during the storm.

KK: Alafair, Dave's daughter, discovers her voice as a writer during the period of the storm, and you mention that she is taking a class at the university that is taught by Ernest Gaines. I am a big fan of Ernest Gaines' work.

JLB: Yes, he's an excellent writer and he's a fine fellow, too. Alafair is working on her first novel at the time. She has just graduated from Reed College, and she's home writing and this bad guy destroys her computer. Dave fears that she has lost her manuscript, but Alafair explains that she emails Ernest Gaines her work-in-progress on a daily basis. So, she hasn't lost it. This practice is one that I use, and so does my daughter, the 'real' Alafair Burke. My real-life daughter, Alafair Burke's new novel, *Dead Connection,* just came out two days ago.

KK: Beautiful. I hope to have her on my show soon. I'm reading great things about her new novel. Jim, the second time I read this novel I began to feel a resonance with some of the themes and metaphors you dealt with in *the Electric Mist with Confederate Dead*, a previous novel of yours that happens to be one of my favorites.

JLB: Thank you very much. I used the true story of a Catholic priest from the lower ninth ward who tried to get his parishioners to leave. But 60% of the people from the ninth ward did not own automobiles. Also, it was the end of the month and most of them had not been paid, and if they had money there was nowhere to go. There was no hotel available from New Orleans all the way to Saint Louis.

But the priest stayed with them, and he drowned with them. I used that story in the book. In the book people see lights under the water near the sacristy of the church where all these people died. Dave tried to discover the source of the light beneath the water; it serves as a metaphor for all the people who were broken and rejected.

KK: And we can never forget those people. On page 245 [hardcover], Dave is talking with Ronald Bledsoe, and Dave says, 'we like to think that we revere Jesus, Mother Teresa, and Saint Francis of Assisi, but when we feel threatened we want the Earp Brothers and Doc Holiday. I thought that was an interesting observation. When we see what happened during Katrina, and watch the images from Iraq and Afghanistan, we feel helpless and that can lead to a sense of rage. *The Tin Roof Blowdown* gives a voice to some of these feelings, it's a moderate voice, but it's there.

JLB: We're at an interesting time in our nation's history. We're in the vortex, so we don't see it all: we're in the funnel itself, but I think it's going to prove to be one of the most dramatic periods in western history.

KK: I think you're right, Jim. You wrote about a letter from the 1960s that was written as an open letter to the Black Panthers by a black pastor in Oakland talking about the importance of the church and the family in black communities. In particular the letter addressed the role of the matriarchal society.

JLB: Yes, the letter was written by a young pastor and his audience was the Black Panthers (guys like Bobby Seale, Eldridge Cleaver, and Hughie Newton) and he said these 'boys' had forgotten that the center of the black community has always been the church. The homes are matriarchal, and the blue collar black families have a very rigid code of protecting one's own. A black family does not give up its own to the system, they will do whatever it takes to protect the child.

Whereas, in a middle-class Anglo-Saxon family, they are more likely to trust the law, and will even go so far as to turn others in to the police. But it is a *de facto* truism that the black community has always taken its leadership from the church. Always.

Politicians always proselytize the church in the black community first.

KK: Jim, I want to tell you that the final two or three pages of *The Tin Roof Blowdown* moved me in a way that few novels ever have. I am not being disingenuous when I tell you that I had to put the book down and reflect on the beauty and the power of the prose.

JLB: I think the conclusion of the book is the best writing I ever did. I'll let others judge that, but it deals with the aftermath of the storm, the people who were lost, the lights that others seem to have seen beneath the surface of the water.

KK: How many times did you write those paragraphs before you got them just the way you wanted to?

JLB: It didn't take long- oddly enough. The words seemed to come naturally at the end of the story. I used the metaphor of a giant pewter-colored chalice, filled with dark water and broken lights in it that were like light emanating from a broken Eucharist. And we remember, of course, the lines in the New Testament; the sacrifice of Jesus was the sacrifice that is broken and rejected by the world.

Christianity is all about rejection, not acceptance. It's always been about rejection. The real lesson and teaching about Christ is always about rejection. He always cautioned his followers to fear acceptance. Those who are last will be first. Those who are first will be last. Christ always indicated that the world will reject His followers.

KK: Thank you for saying that so eloquently. This novel gives respect to those that died during Katrina. It seems that with *Tin Roof Blowdown* and the short story "Jesus Out to Sea" that you are honoring the dead and giving a voice to let those that perished share their stories.

JLB: I think that's what Dave Robicheaux tries to do in all the books. He tries to give a voice to those that have none. I think that's what a good protagonist does.

Ron Hanson said that once. I have a lot of respect for Ron Hanson as an artist and as a man. Ron was asked once why he wrote about people he had never met; people like French nuns living in a cloistered community at the end of the century. He wrote about Hitler's family.

He said that the novelist's 'charge' was to give power and dimension and life to those whose valves are stopped with dust. Ron is an amazing writer. *Mariette in Ecstasy*, what a book! It is one of the best novels in American literature.

KK: Jim, was this novel cathartic for you? Some of the scenes that you describe in the novel are tough to read. You tell the reader that if you get a chance to hear some of these

things to 'walk away' from it- don't embrace it.
These stories must have been emotionally
draining for you to write.

JLB: These are the best books I could write. I
always feel upon completing a book that if I've
done as well as I could, that I have fulfilled the
goal that I have in my life. To tell the truth, at
least as well as I know it, and to put it down in
a way that other people can share in it. I think
that's the greatest pleasure an artist gets.

****

In 2010 *The Glass Rainbow* was published.
Burke called into VoiceCorp, the studio where I
digitally record my interviews. VoiceCorp is a
nonprofit radio station that broadcasts on a

frequency for visually impaired people. They do wonderful work. Chuck Adkins, their head engineer, has recorded and edited every interview that I have done. He has been with me from the very beginning of the website.

I could not have done what I have done without Chuck Adkins. I have no idea what he does; how he works his magic on the recordings we do, but I can tell you that he is the best person I have met at what he does. We have formed an extremely close friendship over the years. Chuck is an accomplished interviewer and announcer himself; I have learned a great deal about the art of interviewing from him.

Chuck has developed relationships with most of the authors I have interviewed over the years. I always arrive at the studio early to do sound checks with Chuck. Then I wait for the author to call in on a private line that the studio has designated for call-ins. This is the number that I give the authors. Chuck and Burke have come to know each other over the years, exchanging pleasantries while they get the recording levels set up.

I heard Chuck say, "Not bad for a blind guy." He was talking to Burke. "Yes, I've been blind since birth. You didn't know that. I'm surprised that Kacey never told you that. Well, thank you, I'm a big fan of yours. I love listening to your audiobooks, but the Library for the Blind usually doesn't get the audio-CDs for a few years, so I have to wait awhile, but I sure do like listening to them. You're a great writer."

I listened to them banter back and forth until Chuck got the levels right. The interview went off without a hitch. Later that afternoon I received an email from Burke asking for Chuck's address at the studio. Unbeknownst to me he called his publicist and had a box of audio CDs sent to Chuck.

Chuck called me a few days later, the emotion palpable in his voice. He asked me if I knew that Burke was going to send him the CDs. I told him that I thought he might, that he asked for his address. He told me that it was one of the nicest things anyone had done for him. He asked for Burke's email address so that he could send him a thank you note.

I guard my 'black book' of author emails and telephone numbers zealously. I had never given anyone's private email out before. It was not that I did not trust Chuck, I trusted him implicitly. I was unsure how Burke would react.

My arrogance and false sense of pride made the assumption that I should protect writers from unwanted calls or emails. I loosened the reigns on my 'control knob' and gave it to him. And that was that.

Several months passed. One day Chuck asked me when Burke's new book would be coming out. I gave him the publication date. He told me that Burke sure was a nice guy, that they had exchanged several emails over the past few months. I laughed at myself and thought back to the day that I had missed James Lee Burke's phone call while walking my dog. *Dreams are meant to be shared.*

****

KK: Jim, this is 18th book in the Robicheaux series, and your seventh time as a guest on the show. Is that correct?

JLB: That's correct.

KK: *The Glass Rainbow* has the feel of a mystery to it. Dave Robichaeux is back in New Iberia and he is working on the rape and murder cases of seven young women. This case is based on a true story. Why don't you tell us a bit about that to start?

JLB: The story of the unsolved homicides is based on real material. Those homicides have taken place in Jefferson Davis Parish between the years 2005 and 2009; they remain unsolved, it's a terrible story. Dave is drawn into this fictional story by his friend, Clete Purcel. There is an amazing level of disinterest in the case because the victims are marginalized people, and they have no voice and they have no power; and unfortunately, that's often the case. Not just in Louisiana, it's anywhere. Oftentimes predators live on the rim of society, they don't have high visibility.

KK: During his investigation Dave leaves his jurisdiction, and visits Mississippi, where he meets Elmore Latiolas. I like Elmore because he just lays it on the line. He says, 'I know who did it, but you didn't care then, and you don't care now', and you show the treatment of these prisoners in Mississippi. There's a beautiful moment in the book where Dave's talking to a prison guard, and he begins to develop a kinship with him, and then he's repulsed by the thought.

JLB: Dave finds himself in that uncomfortable position of talking with a gun-bull, one of the mounted prison guards, who carries a double-barreled shotgun and has killed five men, some on the job, sometimes outside the penitentiary; he killed a man in a bar over a woman. Dave has a hard time talking with this man. He feels that 'redemption works incrementally, but that this lawman is the kind of lawman that all lawmen fear they might become.' A cruel and violent man.

KK: Elmore mentions the name Herman Stanga. This guy is a piece of work. Every time I think you have written about the most despicable character I can imagine, you come along with a guy like Herman.

JLB: Dave despises Herman Stanga. He is a black procurer and dope peddler, and he fills Dave with a visceral loathing: to the extent that Dave never allows himself to be alone and armed with him. Dave despises this guy because of his willingness to victimize his own people. I think it's important to note that all of the characters I create are based on someone I have known or read about. I didn't make them up. To do so would be a kind of manufactured voyeurism. I knew someone like Herman Stanga, he's not a unique character. There's nothing lower, ultimately, in a minority community, than someone who deliberately addicts other people and ruins their lives. He 'literally' steals their souls.

KK: Jim, I believe your attention to detail is one of the things that separates you from other great writers. You give us examples of Herman's life that help explain who he is and why he behaves the way he does. But these things are hard for Dave and Clete to hear.

JLB: We discover that Herman was the son of a prostitute who had a terrible life as a child. But he is not a sociopath, he is simply an amoral pragmatist. We meet some other people in this book who are far more wicked than Herman is. Herman is one of those guys that we allow to function; there's a term for this in anthropology and sociology, 'cognitive dissonance.' There is a reason for every functional aberration inside society. We create a cyst around it, but we allow it to exist because it serves a collective purpose. Gambling, prostitution, the purveyors of dope standing on street corners in minority neighborhoods; these things are all done with consent. Anyone who believes otherwise- well maybe I can interest them in some costume jewelry.

But they're allowed to do these things; this is how we often deal with certain kinds of vices. They are there with permission. Usually they're contained. Certain neighborhoods are offered up as sacrificial parts of town. Think of it this way; the greatest power in any city is vested in the zoning boards. Zoning boards have tremendous power in any urban area. So certain areas are offered up as battle grounds because people don't want to see this behavior in their own neighborhoods.

We let the gang-bangers operate in one neighborhood, but they're not allowed to behave that way in another neighborhood. *De Facto* we've already legalized drugs in this country, but only in certain areas.

I used to live in a slum, I lived in south Los Angeles. It was a great lesson for me. When you see the economics of the 'real world' compared to the economics of a slum.

KK: You also have the Abelard family in *The Glass Rainbow.* I was particularly interested in Timothy Abelard.

JLB: Timothy Abelard is the patriarch of the family. This group of people have a much more pernicious influence on the society and the physical environment surrounding them than these marginal characters do. The people who operate within the dynamics, within the economic parameters of the slum have a minimal influence on our society.

But the people like the Abelards, who are power brokers, people of enormous wealth, in this instance, have inherited an Edenic paradise, the Louisiana of years ago. It was a green, gold creation that James Audubon could have painted. But they traded it all for the short-term gains offered them by the petrochemical industry. And when we meet this family in the book we see the consequence of their choice. They have poisoned the lagoons around their plantation home, the freshwater marsh has been systemically killed by saline intrusion. In effect they have become the serpent in the tree.

They didn't have to go find one in biblical mythology, they were the instrument of their undoing.

KK: As I was reading through the first 100-150 pages I was caught up in the plot and the mystery, all of the sudden I started seeing these very complex love stories developing. The love story between Dave and Alafair [his daughter] is very fully developed in this novel. You do a great job of showing the unconditional love that Dave has for Alafair. She is becoming involved with the Abelards and you do a wonderful job writing about the relationship between Dave and Alafair.

JLB: Thank you very much. Both Alafairs are novelists. The fictitious Alafair, as well as our daughter, Alafair Burke. Our daughter, Alafair Burke, has published six novels now. But Dave has a very trying time as Alafar becomes involved with a celebrity ex-convict who has written a bestseller about his time in prison called *The Green Cage.* And this guy is far more loathsome than Herman Stanga. His name is Robert Weingart- he's just a really horrible human being who Clete Purcell cannot wait to tear apart with his bare hands.

KK: It seems like there is a maturing of Clete and Dave's relationship in *The Glass Rainbow.*

There is a sense of mortality that is developing, and it seems like Dave is beginning to accept Clete more in this book, there is less angst. They're the Bobbsey Twins again. Did it feel that way when you were writing it?

JLB: Yes, absolutely. Certain things we learn in our lives, if we ever learn anything, is that sometime within in the nine innings that we're allocated, we have a few epiphanies. I don't think much wisdom comes with age, it certainly has alluded me, but there are a few things that we grasp somewhere in the seventh inning stretch, and one of those is that while mortality seems to press upon us, the presence of death, its inevitability, but also about this time we begin to realize that death has always been our companion, that it is a lot of what the definition of what human life is about. We were not aware of it, we always saw it as an abstraction, something we would eventually have to joust with, as though somehow, we could negotiate with it.

But when we look back over our shoulder we realized that it was always there, and that our lives could have ended in many ways, in many instances, over the years. Just in a blink- the wrong turn into the wrong neighborhood, a truck veering into our car by veering across the center stripe, a bolt of lightning bouncing off of a power-line. It was always there, we just didn't recognize it as such, and when we realize this we no longer think of our lives in terms of sequence or solar time, we begin to think of our lives in terms of the daily experience. And when that happens people lose their fear of death. It's a very liberating moment, finally. But also, we realize that the moments that had separated us from our fellow man, either though anger, envy, or resentment, those issues just seem to dissolve and blow away in the wind. They are not of consequence anymore. It's the only thing you get with age. It doesn't necessarily come, but that's the one gift- its detachment and indifference.

KK: That was beautiful. Thank you. Jim, I told you the last time we talked about how much I enjoyed the ending to *The Tin Roof Blowdown*. The ending was profound. But with *The Glass Rainbow* you got me again. I am not ashamed to admit that when I finished the book I put it down and wept for five or ten minutes over the beauty of the last two pages. I was a mess.

JLB: Well thanks very much. I appreciate that, Kacey. Louisiana is a tragedy, and it has all of the proportions of an Elizabethan tragedy. It's hard to explain to people how beautiful the state of Louisiana once was. And what has been done to it, or *collectively* what has been allowed to occur there. It is a tragedy of enormous proportions.

The well blow-out at the deep-water Horizon drilling platform was something that I think had been decades in the making. It was the perfect storm. These guys did it- they created the perfect storm. And this is not something that is going to be cleaned up. People who do oil-recovery, who scoop oil and burn it, whatever they can do to dispose of it, estimate a 20% success rate. That's as good as it gets. 80% of the oil that got loose in the environment is in there for decades.

Plus, in this case, the dispersants have sunk the oil out of people's vision, but it's down there on the bottom of the ocean floor, and it's going to be there a long time. And these guys did it. But they did it with sanction, because they provide people with cheap fuel. That's the issue, that has been the issue since 1914, it was the issue in the invasion of Iraq, the invasion of Afghanistan, and it's the issue today. People want cheap gas and if it costs a lot of human blood and sacrifice and misery, unfortunately there are many people who are quite willing to pay that price. Usually at the cost of others, but that's what has occurred.

This is not an opinion. This has been the history of the last 100 years. T E Lawrence's book, *The Seven Pillars of Wisdom,* deals with his experience as a British Commando advising Saudi troops against the Turks out in the dessert in 1915. It's probably the best book written on neocolonialism and the search for renewable fuel sources and what he saw as the future of the western world. It's a brilliant book. If we read that book, we would never do the things we do today. We'd find another way. Anyway, that's the world we continue to live in.

It's an allegory really, the Abelard's are the vestiges of a neocolonial empire. They happen to live in Louisiana, but Joseph Conrad, I think, would recognize them immediately.

KK: On page 242 it appears that you were prescient. You wrote, "and how about oil?" You talked about Louisiana and oil, and this was before the catastrophe on the Gulf Coast had occurred. It sounds like you've seen this coming, being a native of Louisiana, compared to those of us who grew up in different areas of the country.

JLB: You're right, Kacey. I was not prescient though, those of us who grew up around oil production knew how this was going to turn out. That's why there's so much anger in Louisiana, people are really angry. From the day that the deep-water Horizon well blew out, all of the events that followed were a foregone conclusion. There was no way that any other consequence could occur.

And this is why the statements of these men, these oil executives, are so troubling, because they knew better. I voted for President Obama [2008], I think he's a decent and fine man, but

133

he is not experienced in dealing with men like this. They do business with baseball bats, and they were lying through their teeth. Believe me, these guys lied.

At 5,000 feet this was an explosion, not an oil-spill. That was the first lie. An oil-spill involves a leak from a ruptured tanker. Most of the oil stays near the top of the water in an oil-spill. With a blow-out you have an infinite source beneath it, and it comes out with thousands and thousands of pounds of pressure. At 5,000 feet it's a three-dimensional catastrophe.

Secondly, there's no way, effectively, to shut it off. It all has to be done robotically.

Lastly, the damage is systemic, it will last for decades, and in this case the alluvial flow at the Mississippi river, at the mouth, flows directly westward, there was no way in the world that oil could go anywhere in the world except the Louisiana flatlands. You can see the dispersal of the oil from an airplane all the way to Corpus Christi, Texas. In the meantime, the Gulf stream oscillates eastward, that's what I mean by the perfect storm.

The oil executives began stating that 1,000 barrels a day were flowing into the ocean. In reality that number was closer to 30,000 barrels a day (or more.) One of the guys actually got on television and said that the spill would only have a 'modest impact' on the environment. This statement is not only an attempt to hide their culpability, that is pernicious enough; they gave false information to the government about the gravity of the situation. Unfortunately, I don't think Mr.

Obama knows much about the oil business,
the technology involved, but that's not his fault.
His fault is that he didn't get people on board
who were knowledgeable, so here we have the
United States government, the most powerful
political institution on the planet, listening to a
bunch of con men. And that's why people down
south are angry. They have not only damaged
the environment, they have affected people's
livelihood's, their jobs, and their income are in
jeopardy, and they don't see a quick
turnaround on the horizon.

I didn't mean to talk your arm off about this.
But look, over the decades oil companies have
cut 10,000 miles- that's right, 10,000 miles of
canals from saltwater into freshwater marsh
areas. Those marsh areas have been
permanently poisoned. Saline intrusion

systemically kills the root systems both with the native grasses and in the submerged trees (the cypress in the gum of the willow trees that literally knit the land together.) The consequence has been that each year literally 25 miles of Louisiana coast has washed away- it's disappearing- and this situation is going to become more deleterious after the oil surge follows the same conduit into those marshes, and we haven't begun the hurricane season yet. That's when it's going to happen. All that sludge that is sitting on the bottom of the ocean is going right into those Louisiana marshlands, and these guys know that. We need Wyatt Earp and Doc Holiday to deal with these guys. We really do.

KK: I appreciate you taking the time to explain that, Jim. I really do. I loved the line from page 420, one of the guys says, 'this is like *Gone With the Wind,* and the other guy says, 'no, this is like *Suddenly Last Summer* by Tennessee Williams.' And I put a bookmark in the book and set it down. Because he was right, guys like Robert Winegart and Vidor Perkins are like something out of a Tennessee Williams play. I realized that these guys are the grandsons of the characters Williams wrote about 50 years ago.

JLB: Boy, Williams wrote some great plays. Did you ever read *The One Arm and Other Stories and Poems* by Tennessee Williams?

KK: I have.

JLB: The seed of all his plays are in that collection of poems and short stories. Williams' portrayal and point-of-view are very extreme, and we meet these predatory characters. I mean they are literally cannibals. Williams' perspective is pretty horrifying.

KK: It's interesting that you would say that, Jim. Because as I was reading about Robert Winegart I was thinking about Montgomery Clift in *Suddenly Last Summer,* and how Gore Vidal had to take out many of the homosexual references from the play when he wrote the screenplay. I haven't heard you discuss Tennessee Williams before.

JLB: He had a lot of influence on my work, there's no doubt about it. He was a great playwright, and had he not lived in the era he did I believe he would have been a Nobel recipient. I think he was unfairly passed over, probably because of his lifestyle. His behavior was considered outrageous, and he would be considered pretty outrageous even today.

But what a talent! I think that *A Streetcar Named Desire* is one of the greatest plays ever written.

I didn't know that Gore Vidal co-wrote the screenplay to *Suddenly Last Summer.*

KK: Yes, he did. It was in 1959. The play was originally done as a one-act play on Broadway in 1957. then in 1959 Vidal and Williams co-wrote the screenplay.

JLB: I'll be darned. Did you ever see *Orpheus Descending?*

KK: I have not.

JLB: You'd love that play. It's one of his best. It deals with this violent legacy in the south that we often don't want to recognize. It's set in New Orleans and Mississippi and deals with a male prostitute by the name of Valentine Xavier. He was played by Marlon Brando in the film, and I think it was one of Brando's best roles, but again, the themes were so severe that a lot of audiences were alienated by the rawness of the material.

KK: Before I let you go, Jim, I have to tell you how much I enjoyed Tripod, Dave's three-legged raccoon in the novel. Even Tripod is dealing with his mortality.

JLB: Tripod's a great character. One of the themes in the book is the importance of protecting animals. I've always subscribed to the belief that those who do not feel affection for animals are not quite dealing with the spiritual realities that define us.

What we forget when we look into the Bible and we talk about Noah, is that prior to the flood man lived in harmony with animals. The Bible says that 'no knife drew the blood of an animal.' We forget that. That was the world in which Yahweh planned for us to live.

There's also the prophecy about the end of times: that the lion will lay down with the lamb. The Bible has a lot to say about animals and the fact that we're supposed to be stewards and to make the world a harmonious place, not simply for ourselves, but for our fellow creatures. Tripod is a great symbol of that truth.

****

I will end my essay on James Lee Burke with another story about Burke's humanity (and humility). I met Bill Ostrin when I moved to Orlando ten years ago. I met Bill in a social setting and we became close friends. I knew Bill loved to read, but we never discussed who his favorite authors were.

Bill's wife of 50 years died six years ago. I attended her funeral and will always remember the way Bill concluded the memorial service. He and his wife loved jazz, and they loved New Orleans. After the religious part of the service was over, Bill had a Dixie-land jazz band come into the room and they played a rousing rendition of "When the Saints Come Marching In" as the people in attendance exited the room. It was a memorable event.

Bill and I had coffee a few months later and somehow the topic of James Lee Burke came up. I think I had an advanced reading copy of *Light of the World,* Burke's soon-to-be-published novel. Bill told me that Burke was his favorite author and had been for 30 years. I told him about the friendship that I had developed with Burke over the past 20 years.

"How did I not know this?" Bill asked. "Why did you keep this from me?'

I told him my Walter Mitty story about interviewing authors. I knew that Burke's publicist would send me another copy of the novel, so I gave Bill my reading copy to read.

A couple of months passed. Bill read the book with great delight. Bill was an excellent reader. I told him that I wanted him to come up with two or three questions for me to ask Burke when I interviewed him. The next time we met he had completed his assignment and handed me a list of excellent questions. I arranged the date and time for the interview and told Bill that I would like for him to sit in our interview. His excitement was palpable.

What Bill did not know was that I called Burke and told him about Bill, the recent loss of his wife, and what it would mean to Bill if he could spend a few minutes talking with him about his work and his life after our interview. Burke was immediately on board and wrote down a few details of Bill's life that I thought he would enjoy knowing.

The day of the interview arrived. Bill and I had coffee and then drove to my school, where I would conduct the interview. I always use land-lines when doing interviews, cell phone reception is unreliable.

"I'm really nervous," Bill said.

"Relax," I told him, "you have nothing to worry about."

I used a speakerphone that day so that Bill could listen in on our conversation. He was glowing. The smile on his face was priceless. For the first time in a very long time Bill Ostrin forgot about the loss of his wife, if only for an hour.

"Jim," I said, "Do you have a couple of minutes?"

"Sure," Burke said. He knew exactly what I was doing.

"I have a good friend here, the gentleman we talked about. Bill Ostrin. I'm going to take us off of the speakerphone and hand him the phone. I pushed the button and handed Bill the phone. Bill looked at me with terror in his eyes. He put his hands up- indicating he did not want to do it. I told him that I set this up beforehand and to take the phone.

Bill introduced himself and started gushing about how much he appreciated Burke's writing. He called him Mr. Burke.

I sat back and listened, watching James Lee Burke help heal my friend's pain.

"No, no. I can't call you Jim. You're Mr. Burke to me."

Bill stared at the phone, oblivious of my presence in the room.

Burke started telling one of his stories and the next thing I knew thirty minutes had passed. The two men, similar in age, talked about baseball, jazz, the blues, God's grace, New Orleans, and finished up talking about the passing of Bill's wife.

"Fifty years," I heard Bill say. "Yes. I know that you've been blessed with a long marriage too. Pearl's her name, isn't it? Well, thank you Jim. I appreciate your time."

Bill looked at me with tears in his eyes. He now understood what I had done.

I thanked Burke again, amazed at his generosity.

We buried Bill three months ago. I cannot make stories like this up. They happen. A lot of water and hard work have passed under the bridge since that fateful day when I missed Burke's phone call in Columbus, Ohio in 1999.

Sometimes in life reality exceeds the power of a dream.

Part Three

Of Mockingbirds, Tender Mercies,

and a Trip to Bountiful

Horton Foote

I discovered the work of Horton Foote during a dark period of my life. The year was 1983. I went to see a film titled "Tender Mercies" at the Drexel Theater in Bexley, Ohio. The film, starring Robert Duvall as an alcoholic country-western singer, moved me very much. It is a story of redemption, of a man overcoming his past to make a new life for himself. The opening scene takes place in a dusty hotel room in rural Texas. Mac Sledge (Robert Duvall) is waking up from a drunken binge, unaware of where he is or what he has done.

A gentle woman, named Rose (played by Tess Harper), takes him in and nurses him back to health. Mac Sledge was once a star; but the bottle and a nasty divorce from the queen of country music, Dixie (played by Betty

151

Buckley), have led him down a road many have travelled before him. He is bent on self-destruction until he meets Rosa Lee.

Robert Duvall won the Academy Award for his role as Mac Sledge in 1983. Horton Foote won his second Academy Award for best original screenplay. I was 26 years old when I saw the movie. I am 61 years old now. At the age of 26 I did not understand the impact this movie would have on my life. I would never have dreamed that 21 years later, at the age of 47, I would be sitting in Horton Foote's brownstone in New York interviewing him for my website, The Kacey Kowars Show.

In 1983 I was struggling with a serious drinking problem and losing the battle. On January 10, 1984 I surrendered to my powerlessness over alcohol. I had been hospitalized in 1982 and 1983 for alcoholism. I was successful in my professional life as a stockbroker at Merrill Lynch, but my personal life was in shambles. I grew up in the 1970s, and while many of my friends settled down and started families, I did not. I kept the party going until January 10, 1984. Quitting drinking was the best decision I ever made in life. Period. It was not easy, not at all. I had to change everything in my life. But, with the help of many people, I began the process of recovery. I continue to follow that path today.

Looking back, I can see that "Tender Mercies" gave me hope at a time when hope was not a commodity I had much of. I did not understand how the film industry worked, or who wrote the screenplay, but I did relate to the character Mac Sledge at a very deep emotional level. That surprised me. Something in the story touched me in a way that I needed to be touched. It helped me understand at a young age the futility of my situation. If Mac Sledge could do it, maybe I could too.

I had no idea in 1983 that Horton Foote wrote "Tender Mercies". I had no idea that he had written the Academy Award winning adaptation of the 1962 film "To Kill A Mockingbird". I did not know that Mr. Foote did not attend the Academy Awards in 1962 (because he did not think he would win). None of these things mattered to me in 1983.

But in 1984 they began mattering to me. In my new life I began reading voraciously. I had plenty of time on my hands now that I was not drinking (I did not realize how all-consuming the time I devoted to drinking was). I began reading short stories and mysteries. I wrote the short story writer Andre Dubus a letter in 1984 that would change my life forever. 20 years later I started a website where I interviewed authors (I still do that today). It all started with "Tender Mercies".

I met Horton Foote for the first time in 1996. We were both attending the Sewanee Writers' Conference, an annual writing festival held at The University of the South in Sewanee, Tennessee. I attended the conference on six or seven occasions; first as an aspiring writer, and then as a guest, conducting interviews with authors hosting workshops.

I was still a stockbroker during this time of my life. I went to Sewanee to learn to write and to meet fellow writers. I had aspirations of publishing a novel, but writing was, and still is, a passion rather than a profession. I became a high school English teacher 10 years ago. Another good move. I love teaching young people how to write and to read critically. I have had the joy of working with 1,000 young minds, introducing them to the work of my favorite writers.

The first time I heard Mr. Foote read his work I was in awe. I sat in the audience and listened to this gentle, quiet man read a new play he had just finished. He spoke with a Texas drawl that immediately drew me in. He was the quintessential southern gentleman. He was authentic; that much was obvious. He was a fine actor. In fact, he began his career as an actor, but in time he came to realize that his gift was writing, not acting.

I became good friends with the playwright Romulus Linney during this period of my life. We spent time each summer discussing books, movies, and plays. I was unaware when I met him that he was the father of Laura Linney, the fine actress. Though obviously proud of his daughter's achievements, he preferred not to make this fact known publicly, because it inevitably changed the flow of the discussion. In fact, Romulus and I never talked about his daughter, and I know he appreciated that. We talked about his work, which is very impressive. Few playwrights ever achieve the publicity they deserve: it seems to be a part of the creative deal. Horton Foote was one of the American playwrights who did make a name in the theater world, though it was the movies he wrote that brought him fame. It was movies that provided the funds and contacts to write and produce his plays.

I did not have the courage (nor the opportunity) to talk with Mr. Foote the first summer I heard him read. I was intimidated by his humility. Here he was, this paragon of the American theater, sitting two tables away from me, eating dinner and talking with fellow writers. I have met many famous people over the years, most of them nice people. My 25 years as a stockbroker cured me of the idea that rich people lead blessed lives. I admire people that are driven to do what they do in spite of tremendous odds. Those are the people I admire and look up to.

In 1996 I was ready to meet Mr. Foote. I had purchased a video-cassette recording of "Tender Mercies". My plan was to have him sign the box. Looking back now I laugh at myself for several different reasons, the primary reason being the energy I put into 'staging' the signing of the tape. I had become a serious collector of first editions, many of them signed, so the signed box, I knew, held no intrinsic value, but it would be a treasured part of my collection.

The day for Mr. Foote to read his work arrived and I showed up early, tape in hand. I sat three or four rows back in the auditorium. The lecture Mr. Foote delivered that day was titled "How do you do it?" The lecture was brilliant. He talked about meeting Tennessee Williams and asking him, "How do you do it?" He met Arthur Miller and asked him the same thing. He met Eugene O'Neill and asked him how he did it. In time young playwrights began asking him "How do you do it?" At the conclusion of his talk he received a standing ovation, the only time I ever saw that happen at Sewanee. He was genuinely moved. An adoring crowd surrounded him for several minutes afterward. I sat patiently, waiting my turn. I waited until everyone had cleared out and then I approached him.

"Mr. Foote, my name is Kacey Kowars. "Tender Mercies" changed my life in 1983. I consider it a classic, one of the best films made in my lifetime. Would you be so kind as to sign the box of the video cassette I brought it with me from Ohio?"

He smiled that beautiful smile of his and said, "My Lord, son, sit down and let's talk. You were talking so fast that I missed your name."

I told him my name again and we sat there for 15 minutes talking about "Tender Mercies". It was magical. Finally, a woman appeared and asked Mr. Foote if he was ready to go back to his room at Rebels Rest. And just like that he was gone. I had driven seven hours from Columbus, Ohio to Sewanee, Tennessee for just this moment. I went outside into the summer evening and sat for a while, experiencing the feeling you get when something you have really looked forward to happens, and it exceeds your expectations. These moments in life do not come around often, and when they do I have learned to stop and enjoy the moment.

I had met Horton Foote and talked to him about the movie that helped change my life. The circle was complete. I would never have dreamed that night that in eight years I would start my website, that I would call Romulus Linney to ask him for Horton Foote's phone number; that I would fly to New York to interview him in person; that he would finally break his silence about parts of the filming of "To Kill A Mockingbird" with me; that 21 years later I would write this essay- none of that seemed possible that hot summer evening in Tennessee. But all of that, and much more, did indeed happen. This was the first (but not the last) time that reality would surpass my ability to dream. I now know that I was given a gift when I was a child. I had parents that encouraged me to read, and a family that told me I could do whatever I put my mind to. And I believed them.

****

I fabricated a reason to visit Mr. Foote in New York in November 2004. I had gone through the process of getting his phone number (not an easy task) and looked at my calendar prior to picking up the phone. I did have a reason to be in New York. I was still in the brokerage business and could easily fill my schedule tor two or three days. I also planned on interviewing other authors while I was there. I ended up having dinner with Thomas H Cook, and interviewing Lawrence Block at the hotel I was staying in.

I called the number and held my breath when the call was answered.

"Hello". I immediately recognized the voice and made sure I did not rush through the experience.

"Mr. Foote, it's Kacey Kowars. I appreciate you agreeing to talk with me. I consider it an honor."

"Oh, you're very kind," he said. "My daughter came over and I looked at your show on the computer. That's quite a list of writers you have. I believe I saw Tony Hecht's name, is that right?" He was referring to the great poet Anthony Hecht. I had interviewed Mr. Hecht three months before he died, capturing his voice as he read four poems he wrote. The interview with Mr. Hecht was an act of serendipity. I quickly learned to take advantage of situations when they arose.

"Yes, I did. He was a marvelous poet," I said.

"And a very good friend of mine. You know he died, don't you?"

"Yes, I do. One of my goals with my show is to give a voice to poets, novelists, short story writers, and playwrights. I never really understood the power of a poet's voice until I went to Sewanee."

"That's right," he said. "So, when would you like to come over and visit?"

I was ready for this question. "Are you free the second week of November?" I gave him a big target; I would say yes to any time that he gave me.

"Let me see." He looked at his calendar and said, "How does November the 9th work for you?"

"That is perfect," I said. "What time works for you?"

"Let's meet after lunch- say 2:00. You can just come over to my brownstone and let the

doorman know you're here. He'll see you up."
He gave me his address and we exchanged
pleasantries.

"I look forward to talking with you," I said.

"I do too. I'll see you then."

I hung up the phone and booked a flight to
New York.

The world changed forever on 9/11. I
became more interested in books and my
website, and less interested in the financial
markets. It was a difficult time for everyone. I
did not draw a line in the sand and decide to
change careers. It was a natural transition that,
looking back, was guided by a power greater
than myself. I did not know that then. Life is
more easily understood when looking into the
rearview mirror. A brilliant Presbyterian
minister, John Buchanan, told me that one-day

over coffee. That sage piece of wisdom has served me well over the years.

Apple was in its infancy in 2004. Digital recording was not yet upon us. In 2004 I rented a dual-cassette recorder from Hughie's Electronics in Columbus, Ohio to record my interviews. I needed a recorder, a mixer, and two microphones; it took me 20 minutes to put the equipment together before my interviews. The equipment came in a container the size of a large suitcase. It was expensive; roughly $35 a day, cheaper if I kept it for a week. I had to check the equipment at the airport when travelling.

I clearly remember the day I interviewed Mr. Foote. It is memorable for many reasons. I arrived the day before the interview and had dinner with Thomas H Cook after I arrived. Mr.

Cook and I had talked on the phone several times and he became a frequent guest on my show. It started snowing that afternoon; by evening it turned into an all-out blizzard. I woke the day of the interview to eight inches of snow on the ground (and more falling). The temperature was frigid. I left plenty early; taking a cab as far as it could take me. I was dropped off about ten blocks from his brownstone.

I remember how heavy the equipment was (about 40 pounds), and how cold the wind was on my face. I asked myself, not for the first time, what in the world I was doing. Who did I think I was? Why was I spending a lot of money to fly to New York and interview Horton Foote? Did anyone besides me care? Was I changing the world? Or was I chasing a pipe dream, running down a road no one cared about. Moments of self-doubt are normal and healthy when attempting something new and different.

I walked on through the snow towards Mr. Foote's home. I feared that he was stuck somewhere away from his home. Maybe he thought there was no way I would fight the elements to get there. I did not call him after the day we set-up the interview. I respected his privacy and did not want to give him the chance to change the date.

I arrived at his residence at 1:45, 15 minutes early. I tried, unsuccessfully, to thaw out in the lobby. The doorman helped me with the equipment and called upstairs to let Mr. Foote know that I had arrived. He lived on the second floor. I took the stairs and started walking down the hallway. I am sure I was a mess. I had snow, ice, and slush all over my boots and coat. There was no time for a graceful entrance. I saw a head pop out of my destination with a broad smile on it.

"Good Lord look at you," he said. "You must be freezing. Here, let me take your coat. Come inside, I'll put the tea on."

I thawed out and set-up the equipment. I tried not to stare at the framed movie posters, or at the Academy Awards, the Emmy, or whatever else he had tastefully displayed in his living room. He finished a phone call he was having. "Okay, Bob, we'll talk later. I have a young man here who is going to interview me for his radio show."

"That was Bob Altman," he said, referring to the great director Robert Altman.

I was 47 at the time, and not feeling very young, but I was not going to correct him. He was 88. He poured tea and we talked about my show. He was very interested in what I was doing and asked a lot of questions about the rise of the internet He talked about the internet as if it were something he was getting used to yet did not quite approve of. I politely asked him how we were fixed for time. He said, "Oh, I'm not going out today, so we have as much time as you need."

I was prepared for this interview. I spend a great deal of time researching authors before I do the first interview with them. I try to read everything they have written before we talk. I read and watched everything that Mr. Foote had written, at least the things that I could get my hands on. I do not use notes in a live interview. I might write down the names of the characters in the most recent work they had done to make sure I had the details right, but that was it.

I had been warned that Mr. Foote did not like being asked about "To Kill A Mockingbird" [TKAM]. Harper Lee wrote the novel and was famous of her dislike of public attention. She became a recluse because of her fame; she wanted to lead a private life and to be left alone. Readers and the press made that very difficult for her. I imagined that Mr. Foote felt the same way. He wanted to discuss his most recent work, not a movie that he adapted over 40 years ago. I completely understood and accepted that. It did not mean I was not going to question him about the movie, of course I would ask questions. But only after I had covered everything that he wrote prior to the screenplay.

During Part One of the interview I asked him questions about his other work, not necessarily in chronological order. During the break (we agreed to take a break after 25 or 30 minutes) he looked at me and asked, "Have you read everything I have written?"

"Everything I could find," I told him.

"I'm amazed that you did all that from memory. I had forgotten the names of a few of the characters, but you had them."

He had no idea of the time I had spent doing research. The research was exhausting, yet thoroughly enjoyable. I discovered much of his work preparing for the interview. I had no idea he had written so many plays. The plays were what he wanted to talk about, not the movies.

But he understood what I was doing and went along for the ride. He was 88 years old and still wrote every day. I would have guessed him to be 70 years old.

INTERVIEW PART ONE

KK: Welcome to The Kacey Kowars Show, a Celebration of Words. I am honored to have Horton Foote as my guest today. Mr. Foote has created a body of work in the American theater and in Hollywood that includes two Academy Awards, an Emmy, and the Pulitzer Prize. His work has been produced for over five decades now, and he shows no signs of slowing down. First of all, thank you for appearing on the show today.

HF: Thank you for having me.

KK: Mr. Foote probably doesn't remember this, but in 1996 we met at the Sewanee Writers' Conference in Tennessee- which is a place we both hold near to our hearts- and he gave a lecture on the American Theater- about how he had started his career asking other playwrights "How do you do this?" and over time he became one of the writers that were asked "How do you do this?". I cornered him after the lecture and told him that I thought "Tender Mercies" was one of the great screenplays I had ever read, and that it was one of my favorite films [Tender Mercies won the Academy Award for best screenplay in 1993]. Why don't we start off talking about "Tender

Mercies"? How did you and Robert Duvall get together on the project?

HF: Well, I finished the screenplay. Then I called Bobby up, because we had worked together many times, and told him that I had a screenplay that I thought he should consider. I wasn't living in New York then, I was living in New Hampshire, but I had taken an apartment in New York for occasional visits, so we met there. My daughter, Hallie, was friendly with Bob, and the young woman he was dating at the time, so she called him, and he came over. Hallie told me that he could sing, and I didn't realize that. We started talking and I said, "I'm going to read this to you."

I think he was shocked. He had assumed that he would take the screenplay with him and have some time to make up his mind. I'm sure he was thinking, "What am I going to do if I don't like it?" But he liked it. That was the beginning of a long journey- because we did not have an easy time getting it done. We had hoped to co-produce it ourselves, but we didn't get very far with that.

Bob never got discouraged. I did. There were several times when I said, "There's just no point in fighting this Hollywood culture." They just didn't see it at all. There was only one American director that was interested, and Bob didn't like him, so that ruled that out. I sent it to Arthur Penn, who was a very good friend of mine, to Bob Petrie, Delbert Mann, and they just didn't react. In all fairness, I think Arthur Penn liked it; he was, at the time, more interested in a more overt kind of violence.

So, they called and asked me if I had seen the film "Breaker Morant" by a young Australian director by the name of Bruce Beresford, and I said, "No, I hadn't", so I went to see it and I liked it a lot.

So, they said they were sending it to this young Australian director, and I thought, "They're out of their minds. What would an Australian, who knew nothing about culture (so I foolishly thought), going to make of this?"

They didn't listen to me –fortunately- and lo and behold he liked it and they called me and said he was coming to America, and if we got along he wanted to do the film. And we did get along. Later Bruce told me that he only read half of it before he called me. He ran to the phone and called because he was afraid someone else was going to take the job. Little did he know that it had been turned down by a vast board of directors. It's one of those things that I'll never understand. Makes you humble, because it's the last thing I could have imagined for the film., yet it was a great blessing, because he really loved it and understood it. He found a real style for it, I think. He had an interesting way of telling it- so it was a very happy time.

KK: There is a scene in "Tender Mercies" that contains one of the most powerful lines I have ever heard on screen. Mac Sledge has just found out that his daughter has been killed in an accident. He says, "I don't trust happiness. Never have, never will." Did you, as a writer, realize you had written something extraordinary when you wrote that line?

HF: I certainly have learned that it is the line that people retain. I have to say this- it's a lovely scene and I'm very moved by it- but I have to give Bruce and Bob credit for it. First of all, Bruce was so anxious that the studio not fool around with that scene that he did it in one take. And he did it away from the character, so you got the whole thing. There was no stopping it, no running for close-ups. One take and he said, "Let's go", which was extraordinary. And I think it's that utter simplicity that gives it its power.

KK: Let's move on to another film of yours that you did with Mr. Duvall. In this film he sang songs from World War One.

HF: Yes, that was "1918". Willy Nelson sang in that film too.

KK: How did Willie Nelson get involved?

HF: That was the gift of friendship. The man that was scoring the film was a friend of Willie's. Willie had been very admiring of "Tender Mercies" and he and Bob had a friendship- I don't know how deep it was, but I know that Bob was thrilled to sing with him.

KK: I'll bet. Let's move on to "Tomorrow", by William Faulkner, a film you wrote the screenplay for and then produced. Was that done in 1971?

HF: "Tomorrow" had a long history. It was first done on 'Playhouse 90', with Kym Stanley and Richard Boone. And then Herbert Berghoff had a little theater on Bank Street. He loved "Tomorrow" and asked me if I would consider doing it as a play. And I said yes, but who in the world are we going to get to play Mac Sledge? And he said, "How about Robert Duvall?" And I said it would be remarkable if he would do it. Well, he not only did it, but he loved it. The woman who eventually becomes his wife in the play, Olga Belin, was married to Paul Robley, who was the grandson of the Robley family that built the Brooklyn Bridge, and was enormously wealthy. He wanted to do it as a film, and he put up most of the money. I believe we did it for $400,000.

The one difficult thing for me was that he did not want Herbert to direct it. Herman was German, and English was not his best language, so he wanted someone else to do it. I was quite torn, because I owed Herbert a great deal of gratitude, and we had become quite close. He chose another close friend of mine, Joseph Anthony, to direct it. Joe was smart, he had seen the play and Herbert had set most of the acting patterns, so Joe was smart enough not to fool with that. Joe did add some nice things to the film; there is that wonderful scene where she is bathing herself in the sunshine; that was Joe. The two actors in the film had done the play on Broadway, so that part was easy.

KK: I would recommend the film "Tomorrow" to listeners. It's a beautiful story that is well acted and has a powerful ending. It set the stage for many of the things that Robert Duvall would do in the future. Duvall has always been willing to take risks in his career.

HF: Oh my, he's a great risk taker. Always has been. What's interesting, from my point of view, is that I had done, the year before, William Faulkner's "Old Man", which had had a great success; I believe they showed it four times. They had sent it to me and I read it. But I had no idea how I was going to do it. Do you know the story?

KK: Yes, I do.

HF: There's only about two paragraphs in this story about this woman- they don't even name her. They describe her as having a dark complexion, but every actress that had ever played her was a blond. (*We both laugh*). Well anyway, I was walking along the banks of the Hudson, wondering how I would do this, or if I should do it. And all of the sudden I began to think about this woman. I gave her the name Sarah Eubanks, and I just became fascinated with her. So, I did something I rarely do- which is to break apart and redo something- using only half of Faulkner's work. I didn't know him, but he had sent word that he liked "Old Man" very much.

Anyway, I decided to do it, and if the studios didn't like it that was fine. So that's really how I got there. I imagined her, her circumstances, how she got there. And now, of course, she's half of the film. In some ways I feel it's the most powerful part of the film.

KK: So, Faulkner liked the revisions?

HF: I never did know that he did, but yes, he did like it. I heard from his agent. And he did a very kind thing; because it can be done again as a play, or could be done again as a film, although I really wouldn't want to do that. But he's allowed me to share half of the theatrical copyright. I've never heard of that before, and that pleased me very much.

KK: That is wonderful. Let's move on to "A Trip to Bountiful". This was one of the first pieces that you wrote. I believe it was around 1953. Is that correct? Was it written for the television?

HF: It was written for what we called 'live television'. There was no way to successfully record it. It was much nearer to the theater; in other words, you couldn't stop it, and if an actress went off her lines you couldn't prompt them. If you did it would be like giving a line to an actor during a play, the audience could hear it, and they would hear it on the television.

It only happened once to me, and it was Dorothy Gish during her performance of "The Oil Well". She was a sweet lady, but very nervous. I think she was terrified this would happen to her, and it did. She thought it went on for half an hour, but it was only a couple of seconds.

KK: So, when "A Trip to Bountiful" was cast, Geraldine Page won the Academy Award for Best Actress. It's a beautiful movie. Were you happy the way things turned out?

HF: Yes, I was pleased with it. Again, I'm always humbled, because I had about 10 or 12 chances to make that film before. But Lillian Gish did it originally, and she was extraordinary in it. Hollywood didn't think she was bankable. But I turned down 10 or 12 actresses for the role. Let's see- I didn't turn down Betty Davis- no one thought of her in the part, but I did turn down Katherine Hepburn, and all these other people. I just said no. And then Lillian hit 90, and I thought it was time to do the movie. Although when Pete Mattison asked me about

Lillian Gish, I said "No, no, no. She's just too old."

And he said, "Well what if we ask her?" And I said, "No, don't ask her, because she'll say yes." So that's why we didn't use Lillian. And I always felt terrible about that.

I just thought it would be wrong. Because actually, the real Mrs. Watts is in her late 50s. In those days that seemed old. It wasn't the years themselves; it was the life she had led. She had worked hard in the fields; it wasn't the years, it was the accumulation of years.

I know Lillian saw it, I'm sure of that, but she never got in touch with me. And soon after that she didn't remember anything. I guess she forgot that, too.

So, Pete asked me whom I wanted, and I said Geraldine Page, and he said that's who I want. So, we called her.

KK: The film deals with the basic human need of visiting home one more time. It is really a beautiful story.

HF: Thank you. We just had the 50th anniversary of the play [2003]. We had two or three small companies that went all over the country performing it. It was wonderful.

****

Transcribing this interview in November 2017 creates a feeling of nostalgia and euphoric recall in me. I remember seeing the anguish in Mr. Foote's eyes when discussing his 'betrayal' of Lillian Gish. Imagine that, he turned down Katherine Hepburn because he did not want to hurt Lillian Gish's feelings. I cannot imagine this happening today. But it is not nostalgia that is the root of the sentiment; it is admiration for the integrity that Mr. Foote possessed. That type of integrity is rarely found, whether the year is 1953 or 2017. Horton Foote was a gentleman. I count this day as one of my life's 'tender mercies'.

It was a memorable day for many reasons, but I did not have time that day to think about what we had already talked about. I was gearing up to ask him about TKAM. I knew I was standing at the cusp of something great, something important. The timing was perfect. Mr. Foote was 88 years old and he knew I had done my homework. He saw the research I had done, and I knew he would answer my questions about TKAM, because it made sense to do so. It was the natural extension of the conversation we were having. We had another cup of tea, and then we started Part Two of the interview.

I jumped right into TKAM. Why not? I had come a long way and I wanted to know the answers to the questions I had prepared for him. I was very comfortable with the way things were going. I realized that I enjoyed being the one who asked the questions. I was getting better at listening. I learned to ask a question, and then put my tongue between my teeth and bite down hard on it. It kept me from interrupting an author when they were thinking about the answer to the question I had just asked. I learned not to fear the silent parts of my interviews. If the silence lasted too long, we

could edit it out (though that never actually

happened).

****

INTERVIEW PART TWO

KK: Welcome back to The Kacey Kowars

Show- A Celebration of Words. My guest today

is Horton Foote, and we have been discussing

his body of work in the American theater and

Hollywood. Mr. Foote, I would be remiss if I did

not ask you about your adaptation of "To Kill A

Mockingbird", for which you won the Academy

Award in 1962. I've always wondered about

your relationship with Harper Lee. Was there

much collaboration there?

HF: No, there wasn't. I only met her once. They sent me the book and I was working on something of my own, and I really wasn't interested in adapting anything. I knew the producer, Alan Pakula, and the director, Bob Mulligan; they were good friends of mine.

My wife read it and said, "Listen, you'd better get up there and read that book." So, I did, and I liked it a lot. So, I called them and told them I would do it. And they said, "Good, because you're our choice." Harper didn't want to do it. So, they thought that we should meet and see if we got along.

I was living in Nyack, New York at the time, and Alan brought her over, and we just got along well, it was like we were cousins. My town could have been her town, and her town could have been my town. At the end of the evening she said, "I don't want to see you again until you do it." She told me to go ahead. So that's what happened.

Looking back on it, the thing that helped me was… it was a sprawling novel, as a novel should be. It takes place over three years. That was a problem for me right away. I really couldn't find a way to get into the material. There was a wonderful critic called R P Blackmiller, he was a so-called 'high Tony' critic- he was up there in the stratosphere, and he didn't like too many things, he certainly wasn't a champion for popular literature.

He wrote almost an essay review of the novel and the headline was "Scout in the Wilderness". He compared it to Huckleberry Finn. I don't know why that opened the lock for me, but it did, because I love Huckleberry Finn.

Then Alan Pakula suggested that we try to make it one year- rather than three years- spring, summer, fall, winter. That freed me to take on the architecture of the novel.

I re-read it after several years. They were talking to me about doing a play, and I really didn't want to do it. So, I read it again to see if I had been foolish. I had forgotten that there were some wonderful things in it that I did not attempt. Atticus's sister is a wonderful character, but I didn't know then, or now, how to fuse her into the structure of the play. So, I thought, "leave well enough alone".

KK: I understand. When you have something that is close to perfection, why fool with it? Why tempt fate?

HF: Right.

KK: I read in an interview you did that there were changes that the studio wanted to make that Gregory Peck did not like. Did they want to change the plot?

HF: I have no knowledge of that. Gregory Peck was such a gentleman that he wouldn't have burdened me with that. He guarded it closely... the truth of the matter is he saved the film.

KK: Gregory Peck did.

HF: Yes, he did. First of all, the studios were very nervous about it. I think if they had not gotten a star of his commercial power, at that time, that they never would have green-lighted the script.

KK: Were they nervous over the racial overtones of the novel?

HF: I don't know what makes studios nervous. God knows. That's how they are. At the time, you know, Gregory was a well-known leading man. To take on this part was a real risk for him. He had to put on glasses… what really saved it was, and I don't know why he did this, what intuition made him do it, but in the contract, Universal had with Bob and Alan, Gregory insisted on their getting the final cut.

They didn't like the film very much. I'm sure nobody at Universal would admit this, there's a whole new regime there now, but they hated the film.

KK: No kidding!

HF: And they wanted to cut it ten different ways.

KK: The final cut. They wanted to change that?

HF: Yes. But they couldn't touch it. Gregory had the final say. He did not give the power to himself, he gave it to Bob and Alan; they were very young men at the time. It was remarkable.

KK: I think Atticus Finch is one of the greatest characters in American literature. Wouldn't it be a wonderful world if everyone behaved like Atticus Finch?

HF: I think so. I think so.

KK: Let's move on to "The Young Man from Atlanta". You won the Pulitzer Prize in 1995 for this play [at the age of 79]. I remember you talking about the Pulitzer at Sewanee. What have you been working on recently?

HF: Oh Lord, there have been a lot of them since then.

KK: What are a couple of your favorites?

HF: (*laughing*) I like them all. It's like your children. You wouldn't dare name a favorite.

First of all, I had a wonderful thing happen to me, which I wish would happen to all playwrights. There's this wonderful theater called the Signature Theater, when they took me on they had done Romulus [Linney], Lee Blessing, and then Edward Albee. Then I came along. They weren't in their theater; they were actually in a studio way over on the east side. At first it seemed rather primitive, but they did extraordinary work. And that's where "Young Man From Atlanta" was done. The Broadway production was after that.

It was amazing to me. That was the year that David Mamet had a play that I liked very much [The Cryptogram]. It was the play about a little boy whose parents had been divorced. I can't remember the name of it, but it was very moving to me. Then Terrence McNally had a play that was about homosexuality and was considered very daring [Love! Valor! Compassion!]. It had gotten a big response. How they found this little play down here I'll never know.

This guy from Chicago came to see it. Frank Rich, who later became a friend of mine, was on the board that year. He was one of the judges too. I think Clive Barnes was another one. The board recommends the plays. Then a committee of newspapermen, I believe, that make the decision. It's very puzzling; they often choose things that are not well known.

It was that season that restored my passion for the theater. It means the world to me and I just love it. I don't do many films anymore. I would rather do something in a theater off-Broadway than anyplace else.

KK: Is it safe to say that you have done films so that you could write and produce your plays?

HF: Yes! Yes, that's right. That was an enormous boost. They did four of my plays that year. It's wonderful. "Young Man From Atlanta" had not been produced, and they did that. Signature Theater, when they got to their 10th year, asked all of us for a play. By that time Arthur Miller and Sam Sheppard had been done. I did a play called "The Last of the Thorntons".

If it's of interest to you I'll tell you the genesis of that. I find it kind of interesting, because the Alley Theater had called and said we'd like to commission you to do a work. I said, "Well let's talk about it", and I told them I had always wanted to do a version of "The Three Sisters". Greg Young, who's a daring young man, well he's not so young now, said he was all for it. But they had problems with the contracts. It took a long while and meanwhile I'd actually forgotten it.

So, when the Signature called and asked for a play I told them I had this play "The Last of the Thorntons" and that it was not under contractual obligation. So, they did the play, with my daughter, Hallie, and Estelle Parsons. It was wonderful.

It was about three sisters, but two of them were dead before the play started. So, then the Alley called and said, "Where's our play?" I said, "I'm working on it right now." So, I wrote a play called "The Carpetbagger's Children". So, they co-sponsored it with the Hartford Playhouse, which has done a lot of my plays. Michael Wilson was the director. Here again there were four sisters, but three of them were alive. And one of them was dead in the play. I don't know how Chekhov got started in all of this, but he did with all of these sisters.

KK: You can't go wrong when you're thinking of Chekhov. At least I don't think you can.

HF: No, no you can't. So that play we rehearsed it in Hartford, we opened at the Alley, and then we went to the Guthrie, and then we went to Hartford where we had rehearsed it, and then 9/11 took place and I thought that was the end of the play.

So, for two nights we had no audience for it. No one wanted to go to the theater for two days. Then for some reason, he'd heard about it in New York, Andre Bishop [the Artistic Director of the Lincoln Center Theater sine 1992], wrote that he didn't care if he ever went to the theater again. But something kept telling him to come to Hartford, and whatever that is won out, and he came to see the play.

He had his season completely booked, so he did our show on Sundays and Mondays. We were happy to accept that, I don't know how happy the actors were, but it ended out working out for everyone. The next show that Andre had scheduled ended up not working out, so we opened in New York shortly after that time at the Lincoln Center.

KK: You never know how things are going to work out, do you? I'd like to add that your daughter, Daisy, is a playwright.

HF: Yes, she is. My other daughter, Hallie, is an actress. She's been in about 15 of my plays.

KK: That's wonderful. Mr. Foote, I would like to thank you for your generous gift of your time, and more importantly, the great joy, texture, and richness you have brought to the American theater. I wish you continued success in the years ahead.

HF: Thank you, Kacey. You're very kind.

■■■

I spent over two hours with Mr. Foote. Two hours I will never forget. I aired our conversation on December 6, 2004. I divided the interview up into two parts (for a couple of reasons). I was experimenting with the length of time my interviews, and I thought that 45 minutes was too long for one sitting. I also wanted to develop my listening audience by giving them a 'sneak peek' at the second interview, the one with TKAM. Readers can go to my website and listen to both parts of my interview with Mr. Foote for free. I recommend doing that. It will give you the tone and cadence of his voice, his wonderful southern drawl.

I packed up my equipment while we continued talking. Once the interview was over we talked about friends we had in common (most of them from Sewanee). I prepared myself for the brutal weather outside. I really did not care about the weather though. I knew that what had just transpired was another of many gifts that I had been given in my life. I had worked hard preparing for the interview and I was basking in the glow of achieving something rare that might make a small difference in the world someday. A weight had been lifted from my shoulders. I had done it. Money had nothing to do with my new life. I spent over $2,000 of my own money on that trip to New York. I have never regretted any time or money I invested when it comes to my website, or now "A Celebration of Words." Not a penny.

We shook hands. The date was November 9, 2004, two weeks before Thanksgiving.

"Where are you having Thanksgiving, Kacey?"

"I'll be having dinner with my family" I told him.

"Why don't you come over for a piece of pie after dinner. I would love for you to meet my children."

"I would love to," I said, "but I live in Ohio, and I won't be in New York that day"

"Oh, that's right," he said. "I forgot you don't live in New York."

"I appreciate the offer though," I said.

I walked down the stairs, past the doorman, and out into the blizzard again. The equipment was lighter than it had been on the way over. I walked through the blowing snow and thought to myself, "Horton Foote just invited you to have pie on Thanksgiving Day."

Mr. Foote died on March 4, 2009. He was 92 years old. He was 88 years old the day I interviewed him. He was going back to writing after I left him that day. I learned a lot about life from Mr. Foote. He helped me in 1983 with "Tender Mercies". He helped me at Sewanee the day we sat down and talked about his work. He helped us all by writing the screenplay of "To Kill A Mockingbird", and he helped me again in 2004 as I began my journey into my new venture.

I am not much for looking back on the past. I have taken many calculated risks over the years and learned the importance of being consistent in the way I make decisions. Being a stockbroker for 25 years taught me that lesson. Living my life one day at a time helped as well. But I will admit to one nagging thing that I did not do in my life that I wish I had done differently. I wish I had have gone back to New York and had pie with Mr. Foote and his family. I thought about turning around and going back or calling him on the phone when I returned to my hotel, but I did not do that. I left the moment as it was. Like Mr. Foote and I had decided upon, when something is near perfection, there is no sense tempting fate.

■■

This essay has one more story to be told. Three weeks after Mr. Foote died in 2009, I was in New Orleans at the International Tennessee Williams Conference. My website was now five years old and I was in my first year of teaching. Barton Palmer and Robert Bray, two distinguished scholars, wrote a book

212

titled "Hollywood's Tennessee" that spring. The book, published by The University of Texas Press, is used as a college textbook at many universities. Mr. Palmer had asked my permission to use excerpts from my interview with Mr. Foote in another book he was writing about the film adaptation of "To Kill A Mockingbird."

Mr. Palmer and I became friends. He called me in the fall of 2008 to ask if I would interview him and Mr. Bray at the Tennessee Williams Conference to be held in March 2009 in New Orleans. He would send me the book when it was published, and I would interview the two authors about the new book during one of the conference sessions. There would be 250-300 people at our session. I told him I would love to do that. This was my first full year in the classroom. I walked down to my principal's office and asked if I could have that Friday in March off to fly to New Orleans. He laughed and asked me if this was a trick question. I assured him it was not, and he said that of course I could have the day off, that it was good exposure for our school.

Three weeks after Mr. Foote's death I was in New Orleans, meeting many of my literary heroes. I had breakfast one morning with Richard Ford. He took me to a greasy spoon place he knew about and we talked about Raymond Carver. I went to Mass on Saturday night with Frances Sternhagen, the brilliant actress. She had done many of Williams' plays on Broadway and knew him well. The residual portion of Tennessee William's estate went to The University of the South, into a creative writing trust that specified how the money could be spent. It was to be used to support creative writing programs at the university. The money eventually helped fund the Sewanee Writers' Conference (and provides many of the scholarships they offer). The conference, now in its 27th year, is still going strong. A young writers' workshop is now offered as well.

The conference ended on Sunday morning at 10:00 am. The final panel was three people who knew Tennessee Williams. All of Williams' siblings had died, and the list of people that knew him well was dwindling. I knew one name on the panel, John Guare, the playwright, and owner, at the time, of The Strand bookstore in New York.

I had already checked out of my room and was leaving after this panel. The three days I spent at the conference were a revelation for me. The entire French Quarter was filled with the words and works of Tennessee Williams. Thousands of people attended the festival from all areas of the world. The atmosphere was electric.

I wanted a good seat, so I arrived early. It was Sunday morning and many of the people there were nursing hangovers. I was grateful that I was not. I sat next to Ms. Sternhagen and we talked for a moment. A line of people formed to talk with her; so, I began talking to the gentleman who had sat down next to me. He was an interesting man and after fifteen minutes the head of the conference thanked everyone for coming and began introducing the three people on the panel.

After the first two panelists were seated, the third panelist, James Grissom, was introduced. It was the man who was sitting beside me. He was about my age. Two things crossed my mind. First, I was very glad I had been nice to him. Manners pay off. Second, I started doing the math in my head, and could not, for the life of me, figure out how this man knew Tennessee Williams.

I listened with rapt attention as Mr. Grissom told the story of how he met Mr. Williams. When he was 18 years old, Grissom was desperate to get out of Baton Rouge, Louisiana, his hometown. He wrote letters to celebrities and writers asking them for help. He wrote one of those letters to Tennessee Williams.

One day his mother called him to the phone, saying it was Tom Williams (he did not go by Tennessee among friends). Grissom described his reaction when he found it really was Tennessee Williams! Williams invited him to New Orleans, where the two spent over a week together. Williams gave Grissom a list of actresses and gave him the task of finding out if he still mattered to them. He had burned many bridges during his lifetime and feared these women no longer cared for him. It was an extraordinary request of a man so young. So, Grissom set out on his mission.

At the end of his remarks Grissom read a prayer that Williams had asked him to transcribe. Williams went to The Saint Louis Cathedral in the French quarter most late afternoons and prayed. Grissom proceeded to read the prayer to us, ending the conference. It was an amazing moment. When he finished reading the three-page prayer the audience broke out in applause.

I could not move. I had to have a copy of that prayer. I teach my students "The Glass Menagerie" every year, and I needed that prayer as part of my curriculum. I waited for my chance and approached Mr. Grissom. I explained the situation and he told me that he could not give it to me, that it was not yet copyrighted. His book was not yet finished, and he did not hand it out. He told me it would be in his book. I was not going to go away so easily. I continued trying to convince him to let me have a copy. His book, "The Follies of God" would be published in 2015, and it does contain the letter he read that day.

And then, as God is my witness, he looked at my name badge, and said, "You're Kacey Kowars? I'm a huge fan of yours. I listen to all of your interviews. I'm a friend of Daisy Foote, Horton Foote's daughter. Here, give me your pen."

He wrote, "To Kacey, best wishes, James Grissom". He handed me the prayer. I thanked him and walked away in a daze.

On the way to the airport I thanked God for all of His tender mercies. Serendipity. Books have taken me places I never dreamed I would go. They continue to do so. So, I will keep dreaming and refuse to let reality get in my way.

Part Four

Michael Connelly

My sister, Kerry Biondo, called me in the spring of 1991. She was living in Chicago at the time and she had just made a new friend, Ellen Connelly. Kerry and I talked for a while, and that was that. The next time we talked she mentioned that her friend, Ellen, had a brother who was a writer. His name was Michael Connelly. He had a book coming out soon, and she had recently met him. She told me that Michael was quiet, yet he had an intensity about him. She thought I would like him. I cannot completely trust my memory on the dates, but they are close.

I have always been a reader and an avid book collector. I learned much of what I know about the modern mystery thanks to Otto Penzler, the proprietor of The Mysterious Bookshop, located in New York City. During the late 1980s and the 1990s I was a frequent visitor to Manhattan. I was working on Wall Street, and business dictated that I be there three or four times a year. I always made it a point to visit Otto (climbing the spiral staircase to his second-floor office). Otto knows more about mystery fiction than anyone I have ever met. He introduced me to both classic mystery writers as well as up-and-coming authors.

Otto introduced me to the works of Ross Macdonald, John D. McDonald, James Crumley, Ross Thomas, Elmore Leonard, and countless other mystery writers. During one of my visits, in 1992, he told me about a new author he was excited about, Michael Connelly. He handed me a hardback copy of *The Black Echo*. The book had a black dust jacket, with a blue band wrapped around it promoting another author's work. I knew enough about book collecting at the time to keep the blue band, though I took it off of the dust jacket when I read the book.

It was not uncommon for Otto to recommend new writers to me- in fact that is why I went to see him each time I visited New York. I trusted his judgement and he knew my taste. I went back to my hotel room and began reading *The Black Echo*. The protagonist, Harry Bosch, captured my attention. He had served as a 'tunnel rat' in Vietnam. The book's title comes from the sound that the soldiers heard when they were crawling through the underground tunnels. I later learned that Connelly had grown up in Devon, Pennsylvania, and that one of the 'rites of passage' in his childhood had been to crawl through a brick-lined drainage tunnel behind his house. That fear of tight places followed Connelly, and then Harry Bosch, into their adult lives.

The plot centers around a bank robbery; the plot is complicated and well written. It was one of the best first novels I had read. I looked at the author profile page and discovered that Mr. Connelly was an accomplished journalist; that he had covered the crime beat for The Los Angeles Times for ten years, he had been shortlisted for the Pulitzer Prize for journalism in 1986. Now it was beginning to make sense.

My reading skills were sharpening in the early 1990s. I read, on average, two novels a week, and had been reading at that pace for nearly a decade. I preferred reading a good mystery to watching television. I was also traveling quite a bit on my job. Connelly's work stuck out to me. I could see the character development in Bosch. He was a dark, moody man. There were echoes of Raymond Chandler and Ross Macdonald in his prose. I would soon learn that Chandler was his literary hero (as was Joseph Wambaugh).

The Black Echo sold well, and I was not surprised to see Connelly's second novel, *The Black Ice*, on the bookshelves the following year. Connelly is a prolific writer. His literary output is impressive. He has published close to a novel a year since 1992; creating a new series character, Micky Haller, along the way. In July 2017 he is introducing a new female series character, Renee Ballard, in a novel titled *The Late Show.* Ballard will be the first new character that Connelly has introduced in the last 10 years. Connelly publishes non-series books as well. I have been a reviewer for over two decades now, and I can compose a long list of writers who fall into the 'book a year trap', and as soon as that cycle begins, so does the drop-off in quality. It is inevitable. Successful writers become mini-corporations (and who can blame them?).

The number of authors who publish a new novel each year and maintain the level of artistic integrity that brought them a wide audience in the first place, is small. Stephen King is the master of prolific output. He stands in a class of his own. King paved the way for writers like Michael Connelly to do what he does today. Michael Connelly now writes novels, has a hit Amazon Prime series, and has had novels adapted for the big screen- including "The Lincoln Lawyer" (the movie that

jumpstarted Matthew McConaughey's career.)
There is talk that a major network in interested
in developing a television series based on *The
Lincoln Lawyer.*

My sister, Kerry, attended the wedding of
Connelly's sister, Ellen, in 1995. Connelly was
a rising star at the time, but he was still able to
live a relatively anonymous life (most people
have no idea what their favorite writers look
like). Kerry called me afterwards and told me
that she talked to him about his novels, and
she told him that I was a big fan, and that I was
an aspiring writer.

Years passed and from time to time Kerry
would mention Connelly's name, but that was
all it amounted to.

The first interview on my website with Andre
Dubus III aired in June 2004. I flew to New York

in August to introduce myself to publicists and editors. I quickly learned the most effective way to gain credibility with authors and publishers was to put myself in front of them. On that first trip I met with the publicity directors of Simon and Schuster, Random House, Knopf, and Putnam. These directors then introduced me to the publicists that handled the authors I was interested in interviewing. Each publicist handles ten to twenty authors; depending on the popularity of the author, the release dates for new novels, and the genre they specialize in.

I spent three days in New York. I visited close to a dozen people. I had the publishers send the books and galleys they gave me to my house: I was unable to carry them all. I quickly learned how the business worked. I thought I knew a lot about the publishing world, but in reality, I knew very little. I have a great deal of respect for editors and publicists. They are the backbone of the book business. Many of them have been put out of work by the online business model and the collapse of the bookstore industry. I soon came to know and trust several key publicists. They knew that if I said I would read a book they sent me that I would read it and give them an honest appraisal. I never interviewed an author whose work I did not admire.

Occasionally they would call and pitch a new writer to me. They came to know my tastes and listened to my interviews when they were aired. They linked my interviews to their company websites and authors featured them on their home pages. They, more than anyone in the book business, understood what I was doing and how I could help them, and they took advantage of it.

Miriam Parker worked in the publicity department at Little Brown (now Hachette) when I rolled out my website. Miriam was by far the best publicist I worked with. She handled Michael Connelly, David Baldacci, Ian Rankin, Sidney Sheldon, Douglas Preston and Lincoln Child, and a host of other great writers. She was the consummate professional; always quick to respond to phone calls, and to follow through on her promises. She was critical to my success as an interviewer. She granted me access to popular writers that would have been impossible for me to arrange on my own.

Miriam introduced me to Shannon Byrne, Connelly's publicist at the time. Working with

Ms. Byrne was an educational experience as well. She explained the 'art' of selling books and was critical in granting me access to Michael Connelly as his career took off. I believe that if a writer has the skill set and work ethic that Connelly has, there will always be an audience for their work. The situation is not hopeless. It is dire, but not hopeless. Becoming a published writer has never been easy. Publication has always been difficult. The reasons are numerous, but the primary reason most books do not get published is that they are not good enough. Writing is an art. It is a craft that takes many years (and many failures) to reach the level of publication. This fact does not stop thousands of writers from rushing their work into the hands of a gatekeeper before their work is ready (and it never will).

I interviewed Connelly for the first time in May 2005 to discuss his book *The Closers*. It was a crisp spring day, the kind of day that makes living in the Midwest worth the brutal winters. I opened the screen door and set up the dual-cassette recording machine. I checked the levels and then called Michael's number in Los Angeles. We exchanged pleasantries and I told him about the friendship between our sisters, Kerry and Ellen. He was surprised by this and told me that he remembered Kerry and asked me to say hello to her.

My interview with Mr. Connelly that day is memorable for many reasons. He was on the cusp of super-stardom and his ascendency to the top of the world's greatest crime writers had already begun. It was also memorable because I learned a great deal about interviewing an author that day. Connelly is a pro. He is a journalist as well as a fiction writer. He listened to every question I asked him with intense concentration; he was not merely going through the motions. He made certain he understood the question before he answered it. He had listened to a couple of my interviews and knew that I would be prepared for him. I am certain that Miriam Parker had briefed him on the nature of the interview as well.

I started the interview the way I always did, "Welcome to the Kacey Kowars Show, a celebration of words…"

I introduced Connelly and began exploring the character of Harry Bosch. I make it a practice to never read interviews that authors do with other interviewers. I do not want to be tempted to ask a 'good question' or explore an area that someone else has already covered. This is critical to me. The author has most likely answered my question before- I cannot control that. They intuitively know if my questions are rehearsed (they are not) and as a result they bring enthusiasm to each question that might otherwise be lacking.

Here are excerpts from the first interview I did with Connelly in May 2005:

KK: Michael, when you published *The Black Echo* in 1992, could you have imagined that Harry Bosch would still be around, and as famous as he is in May 2005? How hard has it been to stay true to the original character as time has gone on?

MC: No. There is no way you can ever know what is going to happen. No matter where you are, published, unpublished, five books, or ten books down the line, I really believe you have to keep your head down and write the best story you can write and not hold anything back. I went into Harry Bosch hopeful that someone would publish this, not thinking that this would be part of a series, not holding anything back that I might use later in the series. I put everything I could into that book [*The Black Echo*], kept my head down, didn't study the publishing industry, didn't know any agents, or anything like that. I had the book finished before I even tried to look into that world.

And then I got lucky. I got lucky repeatedly actually. Like any unpublished writer, I was in a dark room with a flashlight with the batteries dying. You don't really know anything about the publishing world. It's like this abstract world where you're asking, 'How does this work? How do I get in?' I went to the bookstore and bought a book on how to get published, and like everybody else I sent out lots of letters to agents, hoping that somebody would be interested in my story- interested in me.

On this list I graded them according to who would be my first choice. And though he wasn't the first to respond to me, I eventually ended up with my first choice. That was one of the lucky things. He called on one day, someone else called two days later. I could have gone with that other person. It was serendipity in a way. I'm just glad that things turned out the way they did, because the agent I got immediately had a long view of me, of my talent, of this character that was in the first book, Harry Bosch, and that set the stage that he wasn't interested in being in-and-out, just looking for a deal with that first book where I could be joined with an editor, and I could possibly have a long-term relationship, and it was very fortuitous, because that's pretty much what happened.

There was a little blip in the beginning. The editor that he hooked me up with edited my book and then left before it was even published. A new up-and-coming editor was assigned to me, and he shepherd me into the marketplace, and I've had that editor for 15 books now [2005]. From the beginning, for no real effort of my own, through serendipity, I have had people that had a long-term view of my career- and I know more about the business now, much more than I did when I was in that dark room with the dying flashlight, and I know how lucky that was, because not many writers get that. So that's the beginning. That's the answer to your first question.

In answer to your second question, about sustaining Harry Bosch, that remains, or is, the most difficult thing I do. And I'm not saying it's very difficult, I'm just saying, all things considered, the dilemma of how do you keep a character alive in terms of the reader's mind and imagination, in terms of it evolving, not on the page, not alive with the plot, but how do you keep the people interested in this character?

Part and parcel of that is how do you keep your own interest? There are many similarities between writing and reading, but the major difference, the biggest difference, is time. To read a Harry Bosch book it takes two, three, four days, maybe a week to read. But to write a Harry Bosch book it takes me a year with that character. I have to spend a long time, I have to feel plugged-in and invigorated; able to carry that weight, that water, through the year. And that's where the dilemma is- how do I keep plugged in- and there's no clear-cut answer.

I've tried different things, but the bottom line is that the only constant should be change. Things have to change, have to evolve. I know there are series out there where the character never ages, the reader doesn't know what date or time or year it is, so the character can stay alive forever, but I chose the opposite tact; gave Harry a specific birthdate, the stories take place in that time, that publication period, so

Harry is evolving, he's set against the backdrop of a city that's evolving, and I found that was one way to keep him interesting to me. I make very contemporary use of things; earthquakes, riots, whatever is happening in Los Angeles and build them into the story.

Then there have been other changes, other things I've done. I've taken years off from writing about him. When I write a book that's called a stand-alone, like "The Poet" or "Blood Work", the real reason for that is for Harry Bosch. I've sensed, instinctively, that's it's time to take a year off from him and recharge my battery. Everything I do, all the moves I make, are really for Harry Bosch, and how to keep him going.

KK: Michael, you make a very good point when you talk about Los Angeles. In any good mystery series, the city in which it takes place is critical. California has been the site of several classic mystery series- but I think that Harry Bosch, and what you do with him, combines the craft that Raymond Chandler had with the lyricism of Ross Macdonald, who is an author that I don't think gets the credit he deserves for his influence on the mystery novel.

Ross Macdonald took the crime novel and advanced it forward with social concerns and writing about what was happening in Santa Barbara and the environment. I see Harry Bosch doing the same thing with Los Angeles.

MC: Everyone learns from the people before them. The three greatest influences on me as a writer were Raymond Chandler, Ross Macdonald, and Joseph Wambaugh. What I have tried to do in my books, from day one, was to combine them all. I remember specifically thinking, and this sounds weird, but what if Joseph Wambaugh and Raymond Chandler had gotten together and produced a character, produced a son, if you will? I wanted that to be Harry Bosch. I wanted him to have the attributes of the cop characters that you read in Wambaugh, and of the loner archetype that I think Chandler established the best. And you add in Ross Macdonald and the social mirror that he held up in his books.

I write mystery novels, so I want first, and foremost, stories of intrigue and entertainment, but that's not really enough to suffice, or to fulfill my artistic ambitions. I want to add another dimension. I want to say something about the society that this detective moves through. It might be a small corner of the world, Los Angeles, but if he can do that, if he can make that a kind of 'everyman' story, of how this guy looks at the world in Los Angeles, how he survives, how he gets by, there's an 'empathic connection' that will take you around the world. People don't necessarily have to have been in Los Angeles to understand this character, and that gets into the whole mystery of writing.

It's hard for me put into words other than it's one of those things that you know it when you see it, you know it when you read it, and you know it when you write it- you feel that you're on the same path. I'm definitely the descendant of those masters, and I agree with you, Raymond Chandler is well known- Ross Macdonald is not as well known. I think he took it a step further from Chandler, and I'm endeavoring to be one of the people that carry it forward from there.

KK: Michael, one of the things that I think has had an important influence on Harry occurred in *Lost Light.* That was when Harry Bosch discovered that he was a father. Becoming a father completely turned Harry's life around, didn't it?

MC: Yes, it did. There are now 11 Harry Bosch books, counting the one that comes out in May [The Closers, 2005]. That's one of the most important moments of the whole series, for a

number of reasons, if I can digress for a

moment and talk here for a while.

****

****

It was at this very moment that I realized that

the show I had started, The Kacey Kowars

Show, had a purpose. I had been interviewing

authors for nearly a year the day this interview

took place. I had interviewed my heroes;

authors I had been reading for 20 years or

more. I had interviewed the 'who's who' of

American literature: Nelson DeMille, Lee Child,

James Lee Burke, Jeffrey Deaver, Robert

Crais, Alice Hoffman, Alice McDermott, Tim

O'Brien, Jeannette Walls; all of them literary

superstars. I was the last person to interview

Sidney Sheldon two months before he died. Miriam Parker had asked me to interview Mr. Sheldon to promote his new memoir. He was in ill health and could not travel to promote the book. In fact, his voice was so frail that I could not record it (the only time that has happened). I grabbed a notepad and transcribed our interview. It became the most popular interview I had done up to that point in time.

No money ever changed hands during my interactions with these authors. Sure, I got free advance copies of any book I wanted to read, but the truth was I spent thousands of dollars that first year building my website, renting equipment, traveling to New York to meet publicists and editors (and to interview authors face-to-face).

I used Go Daddy to host my interviews. I paid for a tracking system to monitor my 'hits' and was amazed to discover that through the internet's reach, and the popularity of the authors, that my interviews were being listened to by tens of thousands of people each month, in over 100 different counties. My interviews were (and continue to be) near the top of Google search listings. In fact, the interview I did with Mr. Connelly five months after this interview (to discuss *The Lincoln Lawyer*) has remained near the top of the list on Google's search engine since the week it aired in 2005.

When Connelly asked if he could digress for a minute I knew why authors wanted to be on my show. It gave them the opportunity to discuss their books in a format that allowed them the time needed to fully answer their reader's questions. My format allowed them to go past the 'sound byte' world they lived in. I gave them the time to answer the questions their fans asked at book signings. The idea was simple, the execution was not.

I have always been an avid reader. When I began traveling down the road of developing my website I never dreamed that it would lead to moments like the one I had just experienced with Michael Connelly. I never dreamed that I would sit on Horton Foote's couch in Manhattan and talk about his meeting with Harper Lee to discuss his adaptation of her novel *To Kill A Mockingbird*. I never dreamed that for over 10 years I would interview the author of every book that I read. But these dreams, and many more just like them, came true.

Back to the Connelly interview:

MC: There's a reason for this from a writer's standpoint. When I started writing about Harry Bosch I just kept my head down and wrote. I had no idea whether or not I would be published. But I knew that I would be spending two or three years with him. At the beginning, when you have the blank page, or the blank computer screen, you have no idea what will happen. But I knew that I wanted it to be a good experience. If I was going to go into my room, actually at the time it was a walk-in closet, if I was going to spend four nights a week and all day on one of the weekend days, I wanted it to be worth my time- even if it never got published.

One of the conclusions I came to was to write about someone completely different from me, so that I would have to think what he would do in this situation or that situation. I thought that would make it an interesting experience, so that's how I started down the road of Harry Bosch. And then I got lucky, and there was a call for another Harry Bosch story, and then another. And so now I'm several Harry Bosch stories down the line and it becomes too difficult to write about someone repeatedly who is completely different from me, so over the course of time more of me gets into Harry Bosch and more of Harry Bosch gets into me. He's starting to share viewpoints and attributes that I have. During this period, I became a father. So that turned my life upside down- it made it better. So, I was back to that dilemma of how do I keep this guy interesting, how do I keep him alive, so I decided to make him a father. I jump-started this by surprising him with the fact that he had a five-year-old daughter. At the time I had a five-year-old daughter, so if I needed to do research I only had to walk down the hall to do it. My daughter is actually a year older than Harry's, so I have some lead time on that.

So that's the story behind the story, but within the story it's a huge change in Harry's life. Harry, rightly or wrongly, has grown up in very difficult circumstances. He's been forged in the fires of our failed bureaucracies, going back to the orphanages, the military, the police department, and he has come through that with this idea that he's a man on a mission and that he has a talent, or a craft, or a specialness, and that he's on this planet for one reason, and that's to right the ultimate wrong. To find the people who kill other people. And to do that right he has purposefully, and subconsciously, built himself to be bullet-proof. He cannot be gotten to- he is not vulnerable.

And all that goes away in the last five pages of *Lost Light*. Now he knows that he can be gotten to. He's vulnerable and he has to watch out for someone else, who, unfortunately, does not live with him and is far away from him most of the time, which increases the fear and vulnerability which he feels. It is a huge sea-change and it makes his life more interesting, which I think is the bottom line. It gave the series, and it gave the character Harry Bosch, new life.

KK: Michael, in your new book *The Closers*, you went back to the third person point of view, why did you do that?"

MC: I was in the first person for the past two books. At the end of the eighth book, *City of Bones,* Harry becomes frustrated and quits the police department. Then I wrote *Lost Light* and *The Narrows,* and Harry's working on a 'private ticket' as a private-eye, and when I wrote those books I realized I was treading into the world of the masters, of Ross Macdonald and Raymond Chandler. It took me twelve or thirteen books to get to the private eye novel. I felt that I should follow along the same style, so I switched Harry to first person. I found that to be the big challenge with those books- I was so set in my ways that it was hard to change. When you write in third person you can always hold some things back, but in first person you have to tell the reader what you're up to or you're cheating them. In *The Closers* Harry gets involved in a program that the LAPD really does have where people can come back on a contract basis, or come back full time within three years.

Harry realizes that he made a mistake, and he wants to return to the fold, so he does. So in *The Closers* when he goes back to work at the LAPD I moved him back into third person.

****

****

As I transcribe this interview from 2005 [in 2017] I am struck, once again, by how interested I was in listening to a writer discuss their craft; why they chose the point of view, how they created their characters, how they revised and edited their work. Talking with Connelly that day was a revelation for me. He genuinely wanted to discuss his work in a larger framework than he was normally given.

I soon discovered that nearly every writer I interviewed was interested in taking the opportunity that I was giving them to fully answer my questions. I got lucky.

In the fall of 2005, I interviewed Connelly again, this time to promote *The Lincoln Lawyer*. I read the galleys for *The Lincoln Lawyer* with great interest. Michael Connelly always gets the specific details of a story right. He is a perfectionist. He sat in courtrooms for over a decade as a reporter listening to the dialogue that took place in the courtroom. Writing dialogue is an art form; it is what separates great writers from good writers. The best writer of dialogue was Elmore Leonard. Reading and studying Leonard is a great way to learn how to write dialogue. Leonard was the king. Leonard was once asked what made his books move so quickly. He replied, "I cut out the boring parts and leave in the rest."

Writing *The Lincoln Lawyer* was a risk for Connelly. He knew the mean streets of LA. He drove with detectives in the cities he visited, learning the ins and outs of police work. He talked to detectives and police captains. I have talked to many police officers who refuse to read police procedurals or watch crime shows on television. The primary reason for their disinterest is that they do police work all day long, why read about it at night? The second reason is that most writers do not get the details right; they have not done their homework. But many of these men and women are Harry Bosch fans. Connelly's work rings true with them. In the spring of 2017 the LAPD remodeled their detective bureau's workspace. There is a quote on the wall: Everybody counts or nobody counts- Harry Bosch. This quote is Harry Bosch's personal motto, his mission statement. This is a great testimony to Michael Connelly's respect within the police community. The beauty of the tribute is that they quote Harry Bosch, not Michael Connelly. Details matter.

I remember the day I interviewed Connelly for *the Lincoln Lawyer*. There was an excitement in his voice when he talked about the new book. Scott Turow, the author who revolutionized the genre of the legal thriller with *Presumed Innocent*, had given a positive review of the novel, which was featured on the back of the dust jacket. Scott Turow is a great American novelist. I interviewed Turow in 2010 to discuss the sequel to *Presumed Innocent*, titled *Innocent*. I highly recommend that readers re-read these two novels by Turow. His work is visionary and relevant. His novels stand the test of time. His memoir of the first year of law school *One L* has remained in-print since its publication in 1977 and is required reading for virtually every law student in the country. Having Scott Turow praise his novel was a major break for Connelly. In fact, it was the first 'blurb' that Connelly had put on a dust jacket in over a decade.

Here is *The Lincoln Lawyer* interview from 2005:

KK: Michael, let me begin by congratulating you on the success of *The Closers.* It debuted at #1 on the New York Times Best Seller list. That is a major accomplishment.

MC: Thank you. It has been an interesting and fun career I have had. It's a little bit surprising that 15 books down the line you hit #1, but each book builds on the others, and I had some luck with that one. I know that we talked about it on your show, and I think that helped. We had a lot of TV commercials and a lot of people reviewing the book, getting all the stars aligned, and it all came together with that book.

We've come close a couple of other times, but *The Closers* brought it all together.

KK: Michael, let's talk about *The Lincoln Lawyer.* I think the character you have created, Mickey Haller, jumps off the page at the reader. Haller took a little longer to develop in your mind, didn't he?

MC: Yes, and if you liked the character, and you got a good ride from the book, that's great. It says something about planting seeds and letting them grow. I liked the character and kind of put *him* in my backpack for a while before writing the story. I think my background as a journalist makes me a fast writer. To me, writing is all about momentum. But every now and then I have an idea for a story but it's not the right time to write it. I have to do more research and let the story develop. This book was about five years in the coming. I had to wait for the right time to tell the story. I think the story benefited from that.

Three books come to mind that followed that path, and none of them were Harry Bosch books: *The Poet, Blood Work,* and now *The Lincoln Lawyer.* These three books swirled around in the back of my head while I was writing other books. When the time comes to write these stories it's a wonderful and vibrant experience, and I think that shows up on the page.

KK: Mickey Haller's a defense attorney. How did that work out for you compared to the other books you have written?

MC: It's quite different. It's like I'm writing about the enemy. I'm associated with writing about cops and investigators. And here I am writing about a guy whose avocation is to protect the accused, to find ways to lighten their punishment, or to avoid it at altogether. So, it's a different mindset, but it's refreshing. The fact that it was completely new made it exciting; because of that the writing was shorter in terms of days, but not necessarily in hours. I found myself wanting to write about him all the time. I spent many hours a day holed up in my writing room, much more than I would if I was writing a Harry Bosch novel.

KK: Tell us a little about Mickey Haller. There is a connection with Harry Bosch, is that correct?

MC: Yes. It's not in this book, it's a kind of 'aha'
moment for those who have been riding along
with me. I think I will flesh the moment out in
the future, because I plan on writing more
Mickey Haller stories. When I started writing
this story I thought it was a 'one-shot' deal, but
by the time I was done I liked this character
and knew I wanted to come back to him at
some point.

Way back in my second book *The Black Ice,*
which was published in 1993, there is a three-
page episode where Harry thinks about
seeking out who his father was. He has just
come home from the Vietnam War and he was
at a stage in his life where he wanted to know
his roots. He never knew who his father was.
So, he did the research and found out that his

father was a pretty famous defense attorney in the 1950s and 1960s named Mickey Haller. He had represented Harry's mother on some cases and that was how we was conceived, I guess you could say.

And that's it. It's just a three-page reference-but in those pages Harry realizes who his father is, and that he is dying of cancer. He goes to visit him in the hospital while he is on his death-bed, and then he attends his funeral a couple of weeks later when he dies. Harry stands up on a hillside, far away from everyone during the service, and sees that Mickey Haller had a family, and that means he has siblings, half-brothers, and half-sisters.

Then we jump to contemporary times and this book is about Mickey Haller, Jr., Harry's half-brother. Haller probably has no idea that he has a half-brother who is an LAPD detective, but his name is so distinctive that somewhere down the road their paths will cross, and Haller is going to know that Harry is his half-brother.

KK: Michael, Mickey Haller once said that the worst nightmare for a defense attorney is to represent an innocent man. You explore that idea in *The Lincoln Lawyer.* Could you explain the importance of that idea?

MC: I think the justice system is pretty much geared to process guilty people, basically adjudicating their guilt and what their punishment should be. If you throw someone who is innocent into that process it throws off everything, and if you are a journeyman defense attorney, like Mickey Haller is, it scares the hell out of you.

That's the quote that he picked up from his father: There is no client as frightening as an innocent man. Micky learns that you have to do your best, bring more than your 'A' game, because you can't have on your conscience that an innocent man went to jail because of your lack of skills or because of your mistakes.

I did a lot of research for this book, more so than I usually do, and one of the undercurrents I discovered (though I don't think they would admit this) is that a defense attorney would just as soon not represent innocent clients because of the burden it can lay on them.

I think in popular media and entertainment there are all these wonderful movies and stories about the innocent man that it makes it hard for defense attorneys to deal with, so they shrink back into their expertise, which is negotiating deals, getting the best set of circumstances for their client who they believe is guilty.

KK: One of the things I really enjoyed about the novel is that you interweave several cases into the plot. You give the reader an inside look at how the system operates. And like any great mystery, all of the cases and clues are important. The story becomes very intricate and complex.

MC: I really wanted to do two things with this book. I wanted to show, as accurately as I could, what this kind of life is, which is really about chasing money- getting your clients to pay you. When you see most entertainment when it comes to of the legal system and to trial practices (and this carries over into police novels as well) it tends to focus on one case. The reality is that these guys juggle many cases; cops juggle cases, attorneys juggle cases, everyone is stretched thin.

I like the idea of this guy driving around, kind of floating around the city in his Lincoln Town car, and handling anything he can get his hands on. I got Mickey's motto from a guy I know who says, 'have case- will travel.' He will go wherever he needs to go to make money. That's a big part of the reality of this work, and I wanted to get that into the book.

The second aspect was that I did want to have a plot that was a contraption where various aspects of the cases would come together at the end to show the 'big picture' that was part of Haller's strategy.

KK: Mickey has two ex-wives in the novel. I enjoyed the way you handle the complexity of the relationships. I love the character Lorna Taylor, his second ex-wife. How would you categorize Lorna's role in Haller's life?

MC: She is the office manager of his non-existent office. She's a type of cyberspace character. Mickey's office is his car. He needs to keep moving from court house to court house to keep going with his cases. He needs an anchor, a land-line. Lorna is the one who handles his billing and his scheduling. They communicate primarily by phone. They have a monthly scheduled lunch meeting, but that's not necessary to what he does. At one time they were married, but now they're not. It was an amicable split. It was a second marriage for both of them and they went into it for the wrong reasons and they quickly knew that.

I toyed with the idea of never showing her in the book. But I got some feedback from an editor and some people that read the early manuscript, and they said they liked the character on the phone enough that they would like to see her, so there is one scene in the book, near the end, where she shows up at the courtroom. I still debate whether or not I should have showed her.

KK: I also liked getting to know Earl, Mickey's driver. Music is always an important part of a Michael Connelly novel. Talk for a minute, if you would, about the role that music plays in *The Lincoln Lawyer*. With Bosch it's jazz, but Earl has an influence on Mickey, introducing him to hip-hop and rap (which is the music his clients listen to).

MC: It gets back to the research. I spent a lot of time with a couple of criminal defense attorneys who are on the low-edge of the justice system in terms of who their clients are. Whether it makes a social statement or not, 90% of their clients are from a minority. They are not as callused as defense attorneys are normally depicted. They want to have an understanding of the people they are representing; and these two lawyers told me that I should listen to some rap music, because many of the young people they dealt with were taking their cues in life from the music they listened to.

There's a point in the book where Mickey, when he's slightly drunk, tells one of his ex-wives, that though most of his clients are guilty, that they are not evil, and that there's a big difference. And that's what these attorneys that I hung out with wanted to impress on me, that there is a story behind every person, and that they try to understand their clients and to do what they can for them. And I wanted to get that in the book.

At the beginning of the book I intentionally wanted to portray Mickey as a guy that was callused and only in it for the money, because at some level he is. But I also finessed the dimension of caring as we go along. He takes on the case of a repeat client who he never charges because he has a sympathetic bond for her. He is badly broken when someone he is close to gets killed. He espouses this difference between being guilty and being evil.

The reader has to bear with me a little bit, but it's a slow moving relationship between the reader and the protagonist in this book for the first 75 to 100 pages, but suddenly you'll realize- 'how did this happen? - because I don't really respect defense attorneys, because they're the ones that put killers and drug dealers people back on the street.' But the reader, hopefully, comes to understand that these guys are a necessary part of the legal system and are a part of a 'just society.'

KK: I'm glad you said that, Michael, because I voiced that opinion to Shannon Byrne

[Connelly's publicist in 2005] while I was reading the book. I told her that after I connected with Haller concerning the Roulet case [one of Haller's earlier cases] the book took off for me and I could not put it down. I suddenly realized what was happening.

MC: Yes. I am lucky, I have a lot of freedom because of Harry Bosch. He is my 'franchise case' I guess you could say. I know I have readers that love Harry Bosch and will ride with me and because of him they are willing to give me the freedom to try other things. I know that because of Harry they will have the patience to allow me to 'hook them.' We have developed an empathic bond that gives me the latitude to go off in different directions at times.

Seven or eight years ago I wrote a book called *Blood Work.* There is a hook in that novel that happens on page eight. The hook, if you call it that, happens a little later in this book. I'm not saying 'bear with me' for the first 50 pages- I think the book is interesting and I'm pleased with the story up to the point we're discussing.

KK: I definitely agree. I found the development of the plot fascinating. Michael, at what point did you think 'I really like this character and I think he has a future beyond this novel?'

MC: It was at the point in the book that I mentioned earlier, when Mickey was being driven home by his ex-wife because he had been drinking. They have maintained a good relationship. In spite of Mickey's foibles, she still likes and respects Mickey (and respect is a big part of it) and they discuss their lives, their daughter, his standing in life, and his view of his clients. Everything comes together in this one little scene, it's only one or two pages, and to me it's the best scene in the book, the one I feel best about as a writer, and I came to the conclusion 'why would I only write about this guy one time if this is the kind of message emanating from him?'

I don't have another story for him yet. I'm writing a Harry Bosch book right now, and I thought there might be a place for him in the story, but there wasn't. But I think he'll be back.

KK: That's good news. Michael, am I correct in saying that the film rights to *The Lincoln Lawyer* have been sold?

MC: Yes, they were. The manuscript, when I was nearly finished, circulated around and it was getting a lot of attention. The producers for *Million Dollar Baby* bought the rights. It is pretty exciting. One night I'm watching them win an Oscar on television and then a couple of weeks later I was having dinner with them and they wanted to make a movie about it. It was pretty heady and exciting stuff. There is a screenwriter that I coincidentally happen to know that they hired without actually knowing that he and I knew each other.

Hollywood comes down to one thing. It's not how good the book is, it's how good the script based on the book is. And I think I'm in good hands. We'll wait and see.

KK: That's great. Congratulations!

MC: Thanks. I've optioned a lot of stuff over the years. I've sold a lot of things, but only one film has ever been made from my books. You only have power one time in Hollywood, and that is when you say yes or no to somebody's offer. The rest is out of your hands.

I just told the story about them winning the Oscars, but that's not why I chose them. I had a lot of other offers that I turned down. These guys espoused a different philosophy, and it was one I liked. So, I went with them. I've learned a lot over the years. Books that I thought would be filmed weren't made, for many reasons.

They told me that they were going to write a screenplay with no idea of who would play Mickey Haller when it was written. We want to get the heart of this book into a screenplay and then we'll decide who should play Mickey. Everywhere else I had sold a book they said that 'we're going to write this script for Harrison Ford, or we're going to write this script for Tom Cruise'. They wrote the script with a specific actor in mind, essentially 'baiting' the specific star, and if the star didn't do it the project was dead.

This is what they did with *Million Dollar Baby*. They wrote the script, then got Hillary Swank, and then Clint Eastwood came in at the end. But they started with the script, not the stars.

This will be the first time this has happened with me and I'm excited to see what happens.

KK: That's fantastic. It sounds exciting. Michael, what would you like to tell your readers about *The Lincoln Lawyer?* What are you most proud of?

MC: I'm really happy that I showed another dimension of my skills. I've always been known as a police writer, a guy that writes police procedurals. I'm happy with that, but my roots as a reader go much deeper than that. I have always loved legal thrillers. I date my beginnings as a writer to when, as a teenager, I avoided the heat by going into the air-conditioned library in south Florida. I was sitting on a chair cooling off when a librarian told me that if I wanted to stay inside I had to read something, and she handed me *To Kill A Mockingbird.*

I know that's a great literary novel, but it's also a legal thriller, so I date my interest in legal thrillers back to that time in my life. I also loved and was thrilled by *Presumed Innocent.* I know I've written Harry Bosch books that involve trials and take place in court rooms, but this is the first 'straight legal novel' I've written, and I'm pretty happy with it.

I should be happy with it. It's my 16th book and I try to get better with each book, so I should be in a position where I'm able to write a decent legal thriller, and I think I have. I think my profile, as far as sales go, that there is a slight hesitancy on the part of readers when they pick up a Connelly book and see it's not a

Bosch book. They feel a Harry Bosch book is a sure thing, and they hesitate a little bit when I do something different. This is the first one that I feel there really shouldn't be any hesitation because it's a solid story with solid characters.

KK: Yes, I would echo that. *The Lincoln Lawyer* is really extraordinary when you consider how far you have come with the character Harry Bosch. To start a fresh character like this, who is so different than Bosch, yet is so interesting is quite an accomplishment. More importantly, it is just very well written and very well constructed. It had to be a thrill for you when Scott Turow gave you a blurb for the dust jacket.

MC: I can't think of anyone else I would want on the back of that cover endorsing the book. Turow set the watermark with his books with the mix of literary fineness and the aspect of the legal thriller. He's the top of the game and the fact that he enjoyed the novel really means a lot to me. That was quite an exciting day for me when my editor called and told me that had come in. And if you notice, I haven't put blurbs on my books for about 12 years. My fifth book was the last book I put a blurb on, so to have this on there 10 books later is really exciting for me.

****

I remember the enthusiasm in Connelly's voice that day; the sense that he had written an important book. Michael Connelly, more than any other writer, made me a better interviewer. His keen sense of journalistic integrity kept me on my toes. Our first two interviews, both done in 2005, helped me see what writers wanted to talk about (and as importantly, what my listeners wanted to hear).

I interviewed Michael Connelly seven times between the years 2005-2009. In 2008 I moved to Orlando, Florida and began my career as a teacher. I had taught classes on financial planning to adults at The Ohio State University, Wittenberg College, and Otterbein during my 25 years in the stock brokerage business. I spoke at colleges, libraries, conferences, and corporations during the years 2001-2007 as my website and interest in writing developed. When I told my mother, Rose Marlene Orendi, that I was moving to Orlando to become an English teacher, she said, "it's about time." My mother knew that I would be a teacher one day; she had witnessed and understood my love of books more than anyone else in my life.

My parents were readers, and now, as a teacher, I realize what a gift they gave me. They *modeled* reading when I was a child. My father, Arthur Kowars, Jr., read books like *Cash McCall* and *The Man in The Grey Flannel Suit.* I have had many discussions with parents involving their child's lack of interest in reading. I ask them one question, "do you read in from of them?" If the answer is no, I tell them to start reading books in front of their children. Not on their Kindle or laptop, but an actual book. I picture is worth a thousand words (in this case the cliché is true).

I am drawn to the mystery genre. I enjoy the thrill of discovering a new series. I am frequently asked for book recommendations from my students and my friends and listeners. I dread the "What is your favorite book?" question, but I do enjoy introducing readers to writers I think they will enjoy. I always recommend three or four writers, depending on the taste of the reader. Michael Connelly is always on this list.

A great mystery series creates a timeline that mirrors the world we live in. As society changes, so does the series. The great Ross Thomas (a writer who has been too quickly forgotten) painted a picture of the world he lived in during the 1950s-1970s. History books are wonderful, I read them as often as time allows, but I prefer the entertainment value that a mystery series offers me. I know the protagonist, the secondary characters, the plot lines of previous novels, and I can see the changes in my own life that have transpired since the last book in the series. It is usually best to start at the beginning of the series to fully appreciate the main character's backstory.

In 2008, my first year in the classroom, Michael Connelly came to Orlando to promote his new novel, *The Brass Verdict*. He did a book signing at Urban Think bookstore, located in downtown Orlando. The store's owner, Bruce Harris, had become a friend of mine. I always support local bookstores; my show offers me access to offer promotional events that benefit the literary community. Mr. Harris called me one day in the fall of 2008 and asked if I would introduce Connelly at the book signing and talk a little bit about the modern mystery. I was flattered by the offer and accepted it on the spot. My students were aware of my website (I played them clips of interviews with authors that would help them understand the novel we were reading), but they did not know the extent of my involvement in the promotion of literature. It was my first year of teaching, and we were learning together.

The night of the signing arrived. I told my students that if they attended the evening's event that I would give them extra credit. We read a passage from *The Lincoln Lawyer* in class to whet their appetites. The film rights had not yet been sold. Much to my surprise, nearly 20 of them showed up that night. The bookstore was packed. They had no idea that

Mr. Harris had asked me to introduce Connelly.
I kept that a secret. I was flying under the radar
in Orlando. I was still doing one or two
interviews a month (to keep my website
relevant), but my nights were filled grading
essays and learning how to teach. Learning to
teach was more important than maintaining my
website. Money had nothing to do with it. I fell
in love with teaching. It was that simple.

I will always be grateful to Bruce Harris for
the opportunity he offered me that night.
Serendipity. Over one hundred people showed
up for the reading. My students were excited,
they had never met a famous author before.
Connelly arrived and was seated at the table
where he would sign books. Connelly is a
quiet, reserved man. He has learned the
journalist's trick of thinking before he speaks.

Mr. Harris thanked everyone for coming out to the event.

"I have asked a special guest to introduce Michael Connelly. Kacey Kowars is the host of a talk show that airs on the internet. He is listened to around the world and is an expert on the American mystery. He has interviewed Michael Connelly six times in the past and I urge you to listen to his interviews. They will give you a rare insight into the world of publishing. I have asked Mr. Kowars to discuss Mr. Connelly's work for a moment and then to introduce him."

I rose from my seat and approached the podium. This was pre-Instagram and pre-Facebook. I wish I had pictures of my student's faces. Their mouths were open, and they stared at me in disbelief. I could tell they wanted to ask me questions, like they did in class, but they realized that this would be inappropriate. I discussed Connelly's place in the pantheon of great mystery writers. I kept my comments brief, people had come to hear Michael Connelly, not me.

Connelly stood behind the podium and looked at me. "Kacey are you teaching now?"

I told him that I was.

"That's awesome." He smiled at me and said," Are those your students? What did you do, offer them extra credit?"

I told him that I had, and he smiled again. He had a young daughter and he understood the importance of a teenager's time.

"You guys are lucky to have Mr. Kowars as a teacher," he said.

I sat next to him at the table and listened with great interest as he discussed his work. I had recently interviewed him about *The Brass Verdict*, but his presentation was about the novel *To Kill A Mockingbird,* and the importance it played in his life as a writer. It was a magical evening for both me and my students. It was the first time that I had met Connelly in person and I could tell by the look in my student's eyes that he made a life-long impression on them.

After the reading and the question and answer session (several of my students asked bright, unscripted questions), Connelly began the process of signing books. He had pre-signed a large stack of books, so the line of readers went fairly quickly. Several of my students bought copies and had them signed.

After the line cleared Connelly posed for pictures with my students and answered all their questions. I was moved by his generosity and his genuine interest in my students.

We sat at the table and talked for a while after everyone left.

He told me how impressed he was with my students and how much he appreciated their attendance at the event. He asked me how I liked teaching and I told him that though this was only my first year, that I loved it. I had found my calling.

"I'll tell you what," he said, "I live in Tampa. Get hold of me at the start of the next school year, and I if I can fit it in, I'll come to your school and teach your classes for a day."

"That would be amazing," I said. "These kids are juniors, so they'll be around next year."

"Even better," he said. "just touch base with Jane." Jane is his sister who helps handle part of his schedule and marketing.

"I will be calling," I told him. "Remember, these are teenagers. I don't want to build their hopes up."

He smiled. "I've got one at home. Trust me, I know. By the way, I think it's great that you're a teacher. Good for you." We shook hands, I said goodbye to his wife, Linda, and I drove home in a daze. The evening had gone better than I had ever imagined. It was yet another time in my life when my dreams came up short of reality.

My students were on fire the next day. The classroom came alive and when I told them that Connelly offered to come visit the following year. They knew he would follow through on his promise, and he did.

When the 2009 school year began I asked the students in my class to set goals. Most of their goals, as juniors in high school, were to score well on the SAT and the ACT, pass the AP exam, keep their parents happy, and get into the school of their dreams. These are common and necessary goals for young people their age to have.

"Okay, those are great goals," I said. "I have two goals." I looked around the room and saw their beautiful faces looking at me; they were pleased that I was sharing my goals with them. They assumed my goals would involve their pass-rate for their exam, or some standardized testing measure I had come up with.

"This is my second year in the classroom," I told them. "My first goal is to be the best high school English teacher in the state of Florida after five years. This is year two, so you guys are my second class to help me reach my goal."

The students laughed and looked at each other, pleased that their English teacher had a sense of humor. Maybe English class would be fun this year. Then they realized that I was serious.

"How will you know where you rank?" one student asked.

"I haven't figured that out yet. This isn't ESPN, or the college football weekly poll. But I have indicators that I follow, and I think that last year was a good start. I have a long way to go."

This statement drew more questions. I had forced them out of their comfort zone of the 'curriculum discussion' most teachers have on the first day of class. I stopped them after two or three minutes of questions.

Finally, another student asked, "What's your second goal?"

"Aha," I said. "Someone was paying attention. My second goal is to have the world's greatest mystery writer come to our class this fall to discuss the craft of writing with you and explain how he became a bestselling writer."

Their initial reaction was to laugh again, but this time they took me more seriously.

"Who is it?" they asked.

"Michael Connelly," I told them. I had the most recent New York Times Best Seller list illuminated on the screen in my room. There, sitting at the top of the fiction list, was Michael Connelly. I explained how the best seller list worked, and then showed them my website, where they saw my six interviews with Connelly. Now they were full of questions. "How do you know him?" "Are you famous?" "Why do you teach?" Finally, I stopped them. But make no mistake, I had set the hook. They were on the edge of their seats.

"So, here's the deal," I said. "I'll get Mr. Connelly to come to this very room this fall. What you need to do is prepare yourself for his visit. We need to read his work, we need to understand reading better than we do now, and we need to write. We are going to write every week in class. We'll start slow, 25 minutes at a time, starting tomorrow, but by the time Mr.

Connelly comes, I want us to be writing for an hour a day once a week. Deal?"

They all shook their heads enthusiastically. They were all-in. I gave them a goal, and I gave them a potential reward. It worked. It is my job to create a passion for reading and writing in my classroom. It is my job to make them understand the benefits of being a great writer.

The day Connelly came to my school we rolled out the red carpet for him. We had "The First Academy Welcomes Michael Connelly" painted on the school's entrance. The school library was renamed "The Michael Connelly Bookstore" for the day, and decorated with many of his book's dust jackets. His novels were prominently displayed. He was genuinely moved.

There is one detail from that day that sticks out in my mind. I met Connelly at a McDonald's across the street from my school. He followed me to the school parking lot and got out of his car. He smiled and shook my hand, "Kacey, I have to tell you one rule I have."

"What's that?" I asked.

"I don't tuck my shirt in when I do these talks. I had an editor at the Los Angeles Times that always made me tuck my shirt in. I swore I would never tuck my shirt in again after that."

He was serious. I smiled, thinking how traumatizing school and life can be. Walking into schools always makes adults remember a painful time in their past that involved rules and authority.

"No problem, Michael. You'll be with me all day. I'll make sure no one tells you to tuck your shirt in."

We quickly moved on to his schedule for the day. I had submitted an itinerary to his publicist the day before so that he would be prepared for what to expect. We had a few minutes prior to the start of my first class, so I took him to the library and introduced him to the people responsible for organizing the day's events. He was patient- signing every book- and taking what would end up being hundreds of pictures.

We went to my classroom and I set up a podium for him. The students filed in and were unusually silent, intimidated by being in the presence of a famous author. On the board I had written, "Set your goals high." They smiled.

I had told Connelly the significance of the motto.

Connelly launched into a discussion of reading and writing, answering each question thoughtfully and with great interest. He stopped each time a student raised their hand with a question. One student asked him what his writing schedule was like. Did he write every day?

"Here is what my daily schedule is. I wake at 4:00 am and go into my writing room. I have blackout blinds on the windows so that the sunrise doesn't break my concentration. I write until 8:00 am. Then I have breakfast with my wife and daughter and take my daughter to school. When I get back I write for another three hours. Then I either ride in squad cars with detectives or sit in the court house if there is an interesting case being tried. Then I go home and have dinner and watch baseball, read, or just hang out with my family. I do that seven days a week, no days off."

My students were stunned. Here was a successful author who made a lot of money: they thought he would say that he wrote a couple of hours a day and then went to the beach. I was intrigued with the same questions my students asked. When I was young I assumed, like them, that most people worked until they had enough money to begin backing off of their work schedule. I had a head start on them- I had been a stockbroker for 25 years, so I had a better understanding of what motivates people to acquire more money once they were already wealthy. In some cases, people use money to keep score of their lives.

Their success as a person is contingent upon the numbers in their investment accounts. Others continue working so that they can take care of their families after they die. Others accumulate wealth so that they can support charities, hospitals, churches, and causes that need their help. Others, like Michael Connelly, do it because it is who they are and what they do. Michael Connelly, like many other successful writers I know, writes every day because he loves it.

Connelly continued, "I live in Tampa, but my series takes place in Los Angeles. So, I spend one week out of every month in LA, making sure I get the streets and restaurants right. I need to feel the streets and hear what people are talking about. What music they're listening to. Every detail has to be right. I stay in a different area each time I go, so that I get a different feel of the city. My locations move around; LA is a big city. I do a lot of writing when I'm in Los Angeles."

I was thrilled that my students were hearing about his work ethic from him. They were impressed. The hour passed much too quickly. We had a short break and I got him a bottle of water. He turned and saw the posters my students had submitted for a contest to win a signed copy of *Nine Dragons*, the book that was being published the following week.

Hachette, Connelly's publisher, sent me six copies of the hardcover edition a week before the book was officially released. I decided to let my students create posters for Connelly's evaluation. Ironically, six students put a lot of time and effort into the 'contest', and the work they did was impressive. Thus, all six students received a signed copy of the book, giving them a book, they could start their libraries with. Connelly was impressed with the posters and made sure that I pointed out each student who did the work, personally inscribing the book to them (adding a reference to their poster).

Michael Connelly is a big baseball fan. *The Lincoln Lawyer* opens with Mickey Haller attending opening day at Dodger's stadium. Connelly is a Dodgers fan. One of the greatest pitchers in Dodger history is Orel Herschiser. Connor Jones, Herschiser's nephew, was a student in my class. He looks exactly like his uncle. Connor was in the front row of my second period class. I took attendance while I introduced Connelly to the class. I had forgotten about his love of Dodger baseball, but I noticed him staring at Connor, trying to figure out where he knew him from.

When I finished taking role I told Connelly that Connor was related to Orel Herschiser. Connor told him that Orel Hershiser was his uncle. I never did find out what transpired, but I remember the two of them talking after class. Another small detail that makes a good story even better.

The headmaster of my school, Dr. Stephen Whitaker, had a special luncheon for several of my best writers. I selected eight students (all of whom attended the previous year's signing) to join us for lunch in our school's boardroom. It was a beautiful luncheon. Connelly answered Dr. Whitaker's questions about how to improve our writing curriculum, and then answered the student's questions about what they major in at college if they were interested in pursuing a career as a writer. He answered every question thoroughly, encouraging them to follow their passions.

I have stayed in close contact with every student in the boardroom that day (they graduated six years ago). Every one of them has graduated from college with a degree from a major university. Five of the eight are pursuing graduate degrees. Every one of them has used their writing ability to reach a higher level of success as students.

Meeting Michael Connelly changed the trajectory of their lives. His affirmation of their goals gave them permission to achieve them. That is the beauty of teaching- it allows us to open the pathways to new roads and dreams, to remove the roadblocks that tell young people that they cannot achieve a goal.

I interviewed Connelly at 3:30 that afternoon in our school's student center. We invited parents, families, faculty, and staff members to listen to a live interview that I recorded for my website that day. Over 200 people gathered in the student center. Our tech team set-up the event so that I could send the digital file to my editor, Chuck Adkins, in Columbus that evening. The interview aired on my website, and Connelly's, the following week.

My school did a great job promoting "Michael Connelly Day". Unfortunately, *Nine Dragons* was not yet being sold in bookstores, so we were unable to have a book signing afterwards. It was a long day. Mr. Connelly drove over from Tampa (a two-hour drive), leaving his home around 6:00 am. By the time the interview was over it was 4:30. I had asked people not to bring copies of his books to sign (out of respect for his time). But I knew that they would.

When the formal interview was finished I gave Connelly some gifts of appreciation from our school. I urged everyone to buy *Nine Dragons* the following week. Then someone came up and asked him to sign a copy of *The Lincoln Lawyer*. I smiled and cringed at the same time. Connelly patiently signed that book and dozens of others that people brought with them. I walked up to him and apologized, telling him that I would put a stop to it. He looked at me and smiled, "It's all right, Kacey. Don't worry about it."

We had reserved the front row of the student center for our best lower school readers based on their AR (Accelerated Reader) scores. The kids were not old enough to read Connelly's novels, but they had the childish intuition of realizing that the man who just spoke was important. The head of the event, Dr. Luci Higgins, had placed the students' names on their seats to make sure the interview started on time.

One of the young girls (who I will teach in my class this year) approached me.

"Mr. Kowars, will Mr. Connelly sign this piece of paper with my name on it? I'm not old enough to read his books yet."

I looked at her face and saw a fellow writer, a lover of the written word. I smiled, "I don't think he can sweetheart. Aren't you late for getting picked up?" I offered up a silent prayer that her mom was waiting outside.

"No. My mom said it's okay."

Saying no to a 50-year-old man would have been easy. But try telling a 10-year-old girl that loves books 'no'. I could not do it. With great trepidation I walked over to where Connelly had finally finished signing books. He was now having his picture taken with a host of people.

"Michael," I said. "There is a young girl that would like you to sign the paper that was on her seat. I can tell her no if you're worn out."

He glanced at me over his glasses. "Sure, bring her over."

I walked over to her and told her that he would sign it. She was thrilled, as were the twenty other kids behind her. Connelly walked over to their small circle.

The little girl (I cannot remember who she was) said, "Mr. Connelly, I'm not old enough to read your books yet, but I promise that if you sign this I'll read them all when I'm old enough."

Connelly laughed, then asked her name, though it was on the paper she handed him. He spent time with every child. We finally got back to his car a little after 6:00.

I shook his hand and thanked him for the incredible gift of time he gave my students. I assured him that he had changed lives that day. I asked him to inscribe a copy of *Nine Dragons* for me before he left. I handed him my personal copy of the novel, the copy that Miriam Parker had sent me two months before. He wrote: To Kacey, Thanks for a great day with many great young minds! It means a lot. All best, Michael Connelly.

I walked back into the school and into my classroom in a daze. It was, without doubt, one of the best days of my life. I felt like a chapter in my life was over, that an important milestone had been reached. I put the inscribed copy of *Nine Dragons* on my bookshelf and opened the copy of *The Brass Verdict* that Connelly had signed for me the previous year at the book signing event. I opened the book and read what he had written: To Kacey, thank you for everything that you do. First with your website, and now in the classroom. Keep up the good work! Michael Connelly.

I clearly remember the feeling I had at that moment. It was a combination of fatigue and exhilaration. I felt like I had run a marathon. I feared that my days of teaching were over- that I could never top this day, so why even try?

That thought was quickly replaced by a sense of satisfaction that came from a higher power, a sense of discovering my true calling in life.

My first fifty years were spent chasing money. I am a capitalist; I believe in making money and believe in the profit motive. I believe it is part of what makes our country great. There were months on Wall Street when I made a lot of money. In March 2000, I made as much money in one month as I did in my first year as a teacher.

But I did not feel the warm glow in the year 2000 that I felt that day in my classroom. In fact, I remember feeling similar feelings in March 2000. Was this it? Was holding this check (after nearly 50% had been taken out in taxes) the culmination of my dreams? The end of the rainbow? It felt like it. And in fact, it was for me- later that year the internet 'bubble' collapsed and then on September 11, 2001, the entire world changed. The money I made in March 2000 was gone. The career I had built began to lose meaning for me. That month, with the benefit of hindsight, was truly the beginning of the end for me. But it was the end of something that had never really meant that much to me. Sure, I derived a great deal of satisfaction as a stockbroker, particularly when the market moved higher. I led a blessed life, experiencing levels of success that I never dreamed possible as a young boy growing up in Uhrichsville, Ohio.

The next day, October 10, 2009, there was no bonus check for bringing Michael Connelly to The First Academy sitting on my desk. But at 8:00 am the payoff starting walking in my classroom. Rather than money, I was paid by the smiles of my students, the obvious change in their lives the previous day brought them. They were full of questions about Michael Connelly. They would soon learn that the movie rights were sold to *The Lincoln Lawyer*, and that Matthew McConaughey would star in it. The movie would be released when they were in college. Dozens of them wrote me after they saw the movie, thanking me for bringing Connelly to our school. They told me that their classmates did not believe them when they told them that they had met the author in high school. Dreams do come true.

That was the last time I interviewed Connelly. He became 'white hot' as a writer, and I fell further in love with teaching. Eventually I slowed the number of interviews that I did each year to a trickle. There was not enough time to do everything. But the story does not end there.

In 2012 Connelly published *The Drop*, a Harry Bosch novel. There were only three book signings for the novel; two in Los Angeles, and one at the Winter Park Barnes & Noble in Orlando. The signing took place on a school night in October. I sent Jane, Connelly's sister, a note, telling her I would try to stop by and say hello. She wrote back and said that Michael hoped to see me when he was in Orlando.

I drove to the bookstore and arrived at 6:45. The parking lot was so crowded that I had to park across the street. I was stunned when I walked into the store. The reading was taking place on the second floor, and the entire store was already crowded. I took the escalator to the second level, and had a difficult time finding a place to stand. A table stacked with the new novel was set up in an area that had sixty or seventy seats, all of them filled. Connelly walked out five minutes later to a rousing ovation. It was at that moment that I realized that Michael Connelly was now the King of mysteries. He was, as my students say, a 'rock star'. I was happy for him.

He thanked everyone and looked out over the crowd. He saw me standing in the rear of the audience and waved hello. People around me looked at me, wondering who I was. He then delivered an interesting talk on the status of Bosch's career, explaining the DROP system of retirement for the Los Angeles Police Department. I had discovered over the years that most mystery writers who write series characters allow their character to age. When they are writing their first novel in the series they cannot envision a time when the protagonist bumps up against mandatory retirement ages. This is, in fact, what was happening to Harry Bosch, and Connelly explained the challenges it posed for the series. When his talk was over he answered questions and after fifteen minutes the store manager explained the process that would be followed during the book signing. There was a limit to the number of books he would sign (except for the new novel), and an employee of Barnes & Noble would take all of the pictures- thus speeding up the process. The line snaked through all the stacks on the second floor, extending down to the first floor. I had planned to say hello to him, but quickly abandoned that idea when I saw the line. It was already after 8:00 pm and I had to teach the next day.

I walked up to the manager and asked her if I could say hello to Michael, explaining that I was a friend. Michael saw me and told her that it was okay. I walked up, shook his hand, and told him I loved the new novel.

"Thanks," he said. "I was hoping you would be here. I'm having dinner with a few friends after the signing. They reserved a room at a restaurant for us. I'd love to have you join us, but I'm going to be signing books for a couple of hours. It's your call."

"I'll see how fast the line moves," I told him. People were becoming impatient and I had to move. He nodded his understanding. I went down to the cafe and called my brother, Kurt.

"Kurt, you won't believe this. Michael Connelly just invited me to dinner with him."

"You're kidding!" my brother said. "He wrote *The Lincoln Lawyer*, right?"

"Yea, that's him," I said. "There's only one problem. He's going to be signing books until 10:00. We won't even get to the restaurant until 10:30. I have to teach tomorrow."

"Kacey, it's Michael Connelly! Get ahold of yourself. Get a cup of coffee and go back upstairs and tell him you'll go."

Which is exactly what I did.

I told him I would join him, and then I sat in one of the now-empty chairs and watched while he signed books. At one point a reader asked him," Michael, what writers do you read?"

This is a question that authors hate to answer. The literary circle is relatively small, and writers are afraid they will forget a friend's name or leave out an important book they have just read. In some cases, they do not want to answer it because they spend most of their time writing and do not have a lot of spare time to read.

Connelly mentioned James Lee Burke and Dennis Lehane, and then he looked at me. "Actually," he said, "that guy sitting over there (he pointed at me) knows a lot about mysteries. Tell him what you like, and he will help you out." He returned to signing books.

A small group of people approached me and asked me for ideas. I gave them names like George Pelecanos, Robert Crais, John Lescroart, Laurie King, Thomas Perry, and several others. In fact, I took several of them to the mystery section and pointed out several series writers that I liked. It was fun.

Finally, around 10:15 the signing was over. Connelly thanked me for waiting and I left the store with him and his wife, Linda. I was surprised to see a limousine waiting in the parking lot. The limo had picked him up at the Orlando airport and would take him to Tampa after the dinner party. I smiled at Connelly and said nothing.

"Jump in," he said. "We'll bring you back for your car later." Suddenly I was glad my brother talked me into staying.

We drove to a furniture store located on Fairbanks Avenue in Winter Park. The store owner was a friend of the Connelly's and had catered in a dinner for the occasion. There were seven people at the party. We ate dinner and I could see Connelly slowly unwind. It had been a long and hectic day. His life had changed since I had first interviewed him eight years prior to this, and I was happy for him. He deserves everything that comes his way. After 30 or 40 minutes he asked me to sit down with him.

We found a comfortable place to sit and talk (after all, it was a furniture store).

He told me that he had bought the rights to Harry Bosch back from Paramount Studios. It had been an expensive transaction. He was forced to pay for all of the production costs that the studio had invested. No movies featuring Harry Bosch had ever been released.

Clint Eastwood produced and starred in *Blood Work*, a Terry McCaleb novel, a book that Connelly wrote in 1998. The film was released in 2002. The movie was mediocre and did not do well at the box office. Connelly was not thrilled with the adaptation.

He was pleased with the film version of *The Lincoln Lawyer*. He liked Matthew McConaughey's performance as Mickey Haller. The script stayed true to the novel. The movie did well, and jump-started McConaughey's career (he had recently suffered a series of box office failures). The problem with doing a sequel was scheduling all of the actors, many whom had committed to other roles prior to *The Lincoln Lawyer*. This frustration was one of the factors that led Connelly to use Amazon Prime as the method of distribution for his vision of a series for Harry Bosch.

It is worth noting, for history's sake, that streaming devices were not in existence when I first met Michael Connelly in 2005. The decade from 2005-2015 saw a digital revolution that surpassed anything George Orwell, Ray Bradbury, Neil Postman, or Philip K Dick could have imagined. The traditional forms of media distribution changed, in my opinion, too quickly, leaving the methods of promoting books and movies antiquated before they could react to the change. Bookstores became less necessary as a method of selling books.

We have a new word in our urban dictionary- 'binging' on a TV series. "The Sopranos" broke the mold of how we watch TV. James Gandolfini and David Chase created characters that redefined the genre. Media companies love to copy success, so what has transpired is inevitable. Some shows have been groundbreaking; shows like "Six Feet Under", "Breaking Bad", and "Big Love". The new normal is to buy the last season of "House of Cards" and spend an entire weekend watching it. The writing is better, there are no commercials, and the acting is superb. It is easier to watch 60-minute episodes at home, with state-of-the-art graphics, than to drive to a Cineplex and watch 25 minutes of previews, followed by a movie designed for the children's or teenage market. The primary reason to go to the movies is to watch a film on the big screen or in 3-D. Movie theaters, in the next ten years, will revert back to the larger screen format that was popular in the period between 1950-1990. Bigger is better; small we can do at home (this includes bigger, more comfortable, seats).

Michael Connelly hit the perfect wave. He had a hot property that Hollywood had not ruined yet; he had technology that offered him new options that were previously unavailable to him, and he took a gamble by going with an unproven mode of distribution (Amazon Prime). The weekend that the 'Bosch' series hit the airwaves it was the number one watched show on what we now call 'TV'. It was a smash hit. Season Two was quickly given the green light. Season Three would soon follow. It is not hyperbole to say that Michael Connelly, Harry Bosch, and Titus Welliver changed the world of watching television forever.

That night in 2012 was a revelation for me. I talked with Connelly as he described the options he had for Harry Bosch now that he owned the rights again. We discussed the options he had with traditional movies, along the lines of the 'James Bond' franchise. We talked about "The Sopranos" and the ability to create a show that could produce 10-12 episodes each year. He explored the idea of a television series like Law and Order, with Bosch being the lead detective. The world was wide-open to Connelly. He had the control, which is rare for a writer to have, the money to do what he wanted to do, and the intelligence to do what was best for his readers (and for Harry Bosch). Connelly always puts the fans of Harry Bosch at the forefront of his decision making. We, his fans, have developed a relationship with Bosch, too. The devotion of his fans gives him more clout with producers.

That night, in the fall of 2012, Amazon Prime did not exist, except as the brainchild of some creative genius at Amazon. Two years later he and Amazon Prime would partner in the creation of the 'Bosch' series. Connelly and the producers were patient in the casting of Harry Bosch. It had to be a near-perfect decision. They decided on Titus Welliver. It was a brilliant move. Connelly was always looking for the right actor to play Bosch. The problem, as he discovered with McConaughey, was that major stars would not commit to a series. Their schedules were booked for several years into the future.

Connelly was a fan of Welliver. He said, "The first time I saw Titus on the screen, I knew he was perfect for the role. There was something in his eyes, a sadness and a fierce intelligence that was mesmerizing." In fact, Welliver had recently gone through a dark period of his life, losing a sibling, and then his wife to cancer two years later. Part of the negotiation with Welliver was his willingness to commit to a series of seasons should the series be renewed. He agreed, as did several other lead characters (including Jamie Hector, Amy Aquino, and Lance Redding).

The next brilliant creative move was to release the entire first season at the same time. The pilot and the other nine episodes were released on the same day- catering to the 'binge watching' that had become popular with viewers. Amazon Prime invested heavily in the 'Bosch' franchise, offering a 30-day free membership to new members. The challenge for Amazon was to take older internet users (like me) to sign up to watch a show on their computers or laptops. Those with 'smart TVs' could watch it on their big screen TVs.

In January 2015 'Bosch' premiered on Amazon Prime. I remember the feeling I had when I signed up for Amazon Prime to watch the series. I felt like I was betraying my values, crossing a line that I had drawn in the sand. I clicked on my Amazon account, clicked on the free 30-day trial, and five minutes later I was watching the pilot episode on my laptop. Three hours later I had watched the first four episodes. I was hooked.

The product was stunning. Titus Welliver was the perfect Harry Bosch. Jamie Hector was brilliant as Jerry Edgar, Bosch's partner. The soundtrack was infused with a great jazz soundtrack. Los Angeles looked beautiful and dangerous.

'Bosch' received rave reviews. Amazon quickly ordered a second season. It was a hit. Make no mistake; it was truly a case of perfect timing, catching several revolutionary trends in media and society. But the reason 'Bosch' is, and will continue to be a hit, is because Michael Connelly is the best mystery writer in the world today. Period. It is Connelly's hard work and talent that make Harry Bosch and Micky Haller successful characters, not Paramount Studios or Amazon Prime.

Made in the USA
San Bernardino, CA
26 July 2019